To Michelle—

Well-Come to Retirement

Thriving in Your Third Act

Best wishes,
Helene De Montreux Houston

D1415268

Patricia Peters Martin, M.S., Ph.D.

and

Helene De Montreux Houston, M.S., APRN

Endorsements

"As we live longer and healthier lives, we must begin casting aging as the solution and not the problem. This is an essential message of *Well-Come to Retirement: Thriving in Your Third Act*—that aging can bring wellness across every domain of life, as both a counterpoint and an antidote to the changes and challenges we face. Peters Martin and DeMontreux Houston show us the way and write about inspiring role models who've made this happen. This important book will bring you hope and a practical sense of direction across the third act of life."

—*Marc E. Agronin, M.D. VP for Behavioral Health and Clinical Research, Miami Jewish Health*

Author of The End of Old Age: Living a Longer, More Purposeful Life, *Da Capo Lifelong Books, 2018.*

"Contemporary U.S. culture has a pervasive negative stereotyping of elders, exemplified by using the words 'senior moment' to describe mistakes or faults rather than acts of virtue or expressions of wisdom. This ageist attitude needs to end because it is incorrect and damaging to everyone, regardless of age.

Well-Come to Retirement: Thriving in Your Third Act is a wonderful corrective for negative attitudes about ageing. The authors tell compelling stories of real people and show the unique ways they continue living authentically, being true to themselves, discovering new and different paths of fulfillment, and rediscovering old paths while simultaneously coping with the inevitable reminders of their own mortality and that of their loved ones.

Growing older may not be for the faint of heart, but life cannot be lived fully without smelling the roses and feeling their thorns as well. The lessons about living life to the fullest as we grow old and

'retire' are important for all of us. The authors of this book help us to learn through the inspiring stories of people who make living their lives into works of art."
—*Steven R. Sabat, Ph.D. Professor Emeritus of Psychology Georgetown University, Washington, D.C.*
Author of Alzheimer's Disease and Dementia: What Everyone Needs to Know, *Oxford University Press, 2018.*

"Too many people think of aging as a time of inevitable decline. Even healthcare professionals have a narrow view, based on their interactions with older people who are sick. Martin and Houston dispel these biased views with their stories of elders who continue to live active, productive, and fulfilling lives. They emphasize the many dimensions of wellness which should lead to a much more positive view of later life."
—*Benjamin Liptzin, M.D. Professor of Psychiatry Emeritus Tufts University School of Medicine*

"Finally, a book with the message that we can be more than just a number during our retirement years. *Well-Come to Retirement: Thriving in Your Third Act* confirms our ability to grow holistically during that time in our lives; financially, emotionally and spiritually. This book changed the way I view my retirement years. Now I feel a sense of hope for those upcoming years. I'm not going to lose my identity in retirement; I will strengthen it! I recommend this book to anyone who thinks otherwise. It's never too early to start seeing those years as a time of personal growth."
—*Dr. Lina Racicot, Director of Graduate Psychology, Assistant Professor of Graduate Psychology, American International College, Springfield, Massachusetts*

"As a professional working in the aging population field for nearly seven years, I strongly encourage you to read this eloquent book. This book is clearly a portal to knowledge for everyone who wishes to preserve quality of life in older age. It is perhaps the most valuable book to read while in transition to retirement."

—Dr. Armen Tumasyan, Senior Care Option Manager and Adjunct Professor at American International College, Springfield, Massachusetts

NorLightsPress
762 State Road 458
Bedford, IN 47421

Printed in the United States of America
ISBN: 978-0-9976834-8-6

Book Design and Editing: Sammie and Vorris Dee Justesen
Interior Design: Praditha Kahatapitiya
Cover Design: Kiryl Lysenka

Dedication

To the wise elders who came before us and the people in this book who had the courage to share their stories with the hope of inspiring and helping others through the journey of aging.

Table of Contents

Introduction

Welcome to Well-Come to Retirement
(Helene)

Well-Come to retirement is our way of saying, "Welcome to the third act of your life!" Although retiring is often touted as entering the golden years, from personal experience and as healthcare professionals we realize not everyone welcomes retirement or feels ready for this change. Sometimes this stage of life is thrust upon us too soon, as you will see from the stories in this book.

What comes to mind when you hear the word *retirement*?

Do you picture a man in a tropical shirt sipping a beer while lazing in a hammock; an older couple touring in an RV, taking in the state parks, sleeping under the stars?

Do you see someone attending political rallies or volunteering at a nonprofit organization, donating time and treasure to special causes?

How about a couple who attend courses and lectures at a local college and participate in discussions that challenge their fundamental beliefs?

Then there's the person who never entirely leaves the career she loves, but gradually decreases working hours while staying on top of her game and sharing wisdom developed over many years.

Do you see loving grandparents who have time to spend with their grandchildren, or perhaps end up raising their grandchildren?

Do you picture a retired person without a life partner? Do you see unremitting sorrow, or a newly independent life?

No matter how you visualize your own retirement, chances are you think of people fulfilling their dreams, ticking off items on a bucket list, and staying active in various ways. The key word is **active**. Baby boomers in our society have redefined retirement, based on their desire to continually BE more and DO more.

Thanks to Boomers, the anti-aging industry is a booming business. Women no longer dress like grandmas and the more affluent keep dermatologists and plastic surgeons busy. Aging is a dirty word, not associated with wisdom but with wrinkles, age spots, and flab. Men over 65 strive for Jack Lalanne 6 packs (remember him, guys?). Mel Robbins on CNN (9/29/2017) predicted the global anti-aging market to be over 216 billion dollars by 2021.

With an increased standard of living, retirement has become a career in itself. Leisure activities, retirement communities, and services directed at senior citizens are big business, especially with the baby boomer senior population exploding (25% of the U.S. population according to Forbes.com.) Some refer to this as a Senior Tsunami.

Financial services exploit the concerns of aging adults who worry (with good cause) about outliving their money (think reverse mortgages and annuities). Activities for seniors abound and communities develop programs to help seniors "age in place" and remain healthy.

As healthcare specialists and soon-to-be retirees, we believe staying healthy is much more than physical health. Enter the concept of wellness. In simple terms, wellness means living fully. It is a dynamic process of change and growth, not just the absence of illness. Wellness includes caring for your body, engaging your mind, and nurturing your spirit.

Experts like Dr. Marc Agronin, who embraces aging, and Nancy K Scholssberg, Ed.D. stress the importance of creating healthy, purpose driven lives.

What does wellness look like to you?

In this new world of retirement the choices can be overwhelming, but we believe wellness should be the primary goal. That's why we organized *Well-Come to Retirement* around inspiring stories of people who either mastered the retirement transition, or struggle valiantly to do so. Along with these stories you'll find information and tips from experts on how to plan for and attain the retirement (or not!) meant for you. If you've already entered retirement, this book will give you inspiration and goals for the future.

We centered the stories and ideas around 8 dimensions of wellness that are essential for thriving in later life: physical, emotional, spiritual, social, financial, occupational, intellectual, and creative.

We hope you'll find inspiration in this book and feel "well-come to retirement" as you pursue your own adventures.

The Changing Concepts of Retirement
(Helene)

> *Don't call me a 'senior' unless you're offering a discount!*
> *—Helene*

Baby boomers have developed a new language to define retirement. Much of this new terminology seems like putting a positive spin on the end of life stage—our third act. Why not greet these years with a positive, can-do attitude? An article in Psychology Today states:

> *Boomers 3.0. Instead of heading en masse to retirement communities much like "Del Boca Vista" (the fictional condominium complex in Florida of Seinfeld fame), 60-somethings are going back to school, starting new relationships, exploring their creativity, taking new spiritual paths, embarking on 'encore' careers, forming new communities, fighting for causes in which they believe, giving their time and money away, and yes, bucket listing. For financial and other reasons, a good number are working and staying in their current homes as long as possible, seeing no compelling reason to do otherwise.*

Today, baby boomers are writing their own rules for retirement. Continuing to find meaning and purpose in life seems to be the underlying goal for most of us, but each retirement is personally defined. As a group we're tossing out the predefined roles and expectations of society and following our own paths. Regarding this life transition, expert Dr. Nancy Schlossberg identified six categories of retirees, based on their paths to retirement. In her book *Revitalizing Retirement: Reshaping you Identity, Relationships and Purpose*, she describes retirees as:

- **Continuers** who still identify with their previous work, home or volunteer life;
- **Easy Gliders** who take each day as it comes;
- **Adventurers** who make daring changes to their lives;
- **Searchers** who haven't yet found the right new path;
- **Involved Spectators**, still involved with their previous work;
- **Retreaters**, who avoid participating in retirement and may just need a time out.

Throughout this book we'll refer to these types of older citizens; not to label them, but to explain the attitudes, challenges, setbacks, and triumphs of people who are creating new paradigms for aging.

Wellness and Retirement
(Patricia)

Wellness, a word that became popular in the 1980's, has gained such popularity that we find it on medical buildings, behavioral health sites, work-out facilities, and ads for dozens of products. It seems everyone wants wellness—but what does wellness actually mean, and is it a new concept?

Although we have no universally accepted definition of wellness, The World Health Organization defines wellness as "...a state of complete physical, mental, and social well-being, and not merely the absence of disease or infirmity."

Like the WHO model, almost all definitions of wellness include finding balance in our mental, physical, and spiritual lives. This concept was recognized by the Roman statesman Cicero in the following essay titled "De Senectute" in 44 B.C.:

> *It is our duty, my young friends, to resist old age; to compensate for its defects by a watchful care; to fight against it as we would fight against disease...to adopt a regimen of health: to practice moderate exercise; and to take just enough food and drink to restore our strength and not to overburden it. Nor, indeed are we to give our attention solely to the body; much greater care is due to the mind and soul; for they, too, like lamps grow dim with time, unless we keep them supplied with oil.*

Before Cicero's time the Greek philosopher Aristotle (384-322 B.C.) created an ethical doctrine of how humans should live. He stressed the importance of moderation, balance, friendship, and intellectual virtues for a fulfilling life.

If great philosophers contemplated wellness and well-being over 2000 years ago, who are we to reinvent the wheel? Rather, we will embrace the age-old concept of wellness as we plan our retirements and contemplate what lies ahead.

Our model of wellness for this book is the definition of wellness used at the University of California, Davis: "Wellness is an active process of becoming aware of and making choices toward a healthy and fulfilling life. Wellness is more than being free from illness; it is a dynamic process of change and growth."

Well-Come to Retirement is organized around the 8 dimensions of wellness and illustrated by life stories of people whose lives illustrate this dynamic process:

Social Wellness: relating to and connecting with other people in a meaningful way.

Emotional/Mental Wellness: understanding and accepting our feelings and coping with life challenges.

Spiritual Wellness: establishing peace, harmony and balance in our lives as we seek meaning and purpose in human existence.

Occupational Wellness: gaining personal fulfillment from work or volunteer activities that use our unique gifts, skill, and talents.

Intellectual Wellness: keeping our minds open to new ideas and experiences as we pursue lifelong learning opportunities and stimulating mental activities.

Creative Wellness: maintaining or tapping into our creative, artistic side.

Financial Wellness: managing our finances so that we can live within our means.

Physical Wellness: maintaining a healthy quality of life while avoiding destructive habits.

Well-come to Retirement is the first book that brings together research, current literature, and personal stories of wellness during the retirement years. You'll read about real people who grabbed the reins of retirement and took themselves on an exciting ride. These are people who learned to reengage and reenter life with new purpose and meaning—people who feel ageless regardless of aging.

May these stories stir you to action and help you find joy and wellness in your life.

NOTES

Samuel R Lawrence, Ph.D., "The New and Improved Third Act of Life," *Psychology Today*, April 13, 2017.

Nancy Schlossberg, M.D., *Revitalizing Retirement: Reshaping you Identity, Relationships and Purpose,* (Lifetools; 1 edition, February 15, 2009).

Cicero, trans. 1946, by W.A. Falconer, Cambridge, MA., Harvard University Press.

Social Wellness

I Had to Reinvent Myself

Dianne

(Helene)

> *"Life isn't about finding yourself. Life is about creating yourself." — George Bernard Shaw*

Upon hearing about a woman who fears retirement at the age of 84, my friend Dianne said, "She'll need to reinvent herself. That's what I did."

Dianne is now 75 and loves retirement, but the first night alone in her new home after spending three months with her son's family was a difficult one. She lay awake, feeling sad, anxious, and lost. She told herself, "I don't know a single person here and I have no friends."

But the next morning Dianne sprang into action—planning her new life just as she planned things before retirement. This is Dianne's story:

The two of us met in the 1970's while working as staff nurses in a psychiatric unit. Dianne was long and lean with straight brown hair halfway down her back (remember, this was the 1970s!). Her bright blue eyes sparkled and her smile could melt hearts. She had just returned to the area after accompanying her husband to complete his graduate work. I was pregnant with my first child and Dianne would soon have two of her own. After that period of time our paths crossed every so often, with uproarious, irreverent laughter as the common denominator.

Dianne is one of the brightest people I've ever met and would have been an excellent physician. She told her guidance counselor in high school, "I love math and science—maybe I can be a doctor."

"Oh, no," the counselor said, "You're a girl. You'll have to be a nurse." During those years, medical and veterinary schools only accepted about 1% female students. No one encouraged this extraordinarily bright young woman to reach for the stars, so Dianne attended a hospital school of nursing. She received an excellent education and excelled in her career, but found it difficult to advance in nursing because credits from hospital nursing schools weren't accepted by universities. Thankfully, this would change many years later, but too late for Dianne and other women of her era. Had Dianne been born 50 years later she could have been a physician or a Ph.D. nurse.

I'll never forget a defining moment that showed me exactly how bright Dianne is: We were on duty during a quiet shift in the emergency room; our beepers made nary a tweet. I sat at the desk cutting coupons and writing Christmas cards. Dianne sat quietly on the couch reading a book on quantum theory—for pleasure!

At one point in our careers Dianne and I founded a women's therapy/support group—a weekly meeting for women going through depression, anxiety, and other problems in response to divorce. Little did I know, around this time Dianne's own marriage was unraveling.

This amazed me because Dianne was the best wife I could imagine. She was capable of handling any emergency (ER nurse), physically strong and energetic, and beyond nurturing. I knew her as a loving and conscientious parent who made sure home cooked food was on the table regardless of her work schedule and level of fatigue. Sadly, she has never remarried. As her friend, I tend to think no man is worthy of her.

Dianne managed two bright and active children through teenage challenges and college acceptances. Her children reflect her intellect and she mastered the art of scrimping and saving so her son and daughter could attend prestigious universities.

Meanwhile, Dianne's career evolved to the psychiatric consultation-liaison service at a large medical center. Her warm and engaging personality, knowledge, expertise, and compassionate approach to patients made her a beloved member of the medical team.

Around age 62, the cumulative miles she walked between medical units began talking a toll on Dianne's energy and joints. She said, "If I wore a Fit Bit it would've exploded. I started thinking hard about retirement.

"I wanted to keep living in the townhouse I'd owned and loved for 16 years, but I knew I'd probably need a chairlift at some point. I definitely wanted to stay active with my church, friends, and extended family."

She continues, "After the children finished college I had started a retirement fund in a 403B through the medical center. That, plus my pension and social security would help me survive and thrive in a financial way."

During those years Dianne planned for the future by deliberately "living lean." She clipped coupons, shopped at sales, and "never paid full price." She also consulted a financial planner who helped her money grow.

Seeing her father pass away and leave her mother with no income or savings was a wake-up call. Her mother found a job she loved, but this was a life lesson Dianne never forgot.

Saving for retirement doesn't have to take all the fun out of life, Dianne says. "I still enjoyed myself while saving. I especially love going to symphony concerts and I took some wonderful trips. I visited India five times, where I still have friends from when I was an exchange student. I looked forward to spending my so-called golden years in New England."

However, the best laid plans are subject to change.

When she made the decision to retire, Dianne's son said, "Mom, why don't you come to California and live near us?" The warm California climate would soothe her aching joints and Dianne loved being close to family.

A psychiatrist friend told her, "When you retire, you need to do something different with your life." Dianne quickly followed that advice and headed west on a new adventure. Her son helped with the finances and she now lives in a lovely retirement home in Half Moon Bay with lifetime tenancy. Dianne recalls this time:

I have to admit I felt lonely and frightened at first. My familiar home was gone, my friends were far away, and even the climate seemed strange.

"But I took action before those feelings could rule my life. I made an effort to meet new friends and looked for places to volunteer as a nurse, because I soon started missing my profession. I actually mourned not being a nurse. There's nothing like the intimacy between a nurse and her patient. I asked a few questions and soon became a volunteer nurse for the Medical Reserve Corps."

Dianne is also president of the board of directors of Coastside Hope, a non-profit serving the needy along the San Mateo County Coastline. She tells me, "I'm proud to say we have over 3,000 client visits per year and provide food, lodging, and other services for immigrants at risk." She also worked as a volunteer docent for the historic Johnston House, a beautiful antique saltbox home near where Dianne lives. The home reminded her of her beloved New England. Warm friendships have developed from these volunteer efforts and associations. One of her friends introduced her to Buzztime—a weekly trivia competition at the local family pub. Dianne's equally brilliant brother lives in San Francisco and joins her for the weekly Buzztime. He is another ringer, and let it be said they "kill it!"

Dianne's California retreat is filled with memorabilia from her trips to India, has a beautiful guest suite that encourages her many friends to visit, and a yard filled with flowers, lemons trees, and hummingbirds. Her son is 20 minutes away and Dianne fills her home with family celebrations whenever possible.

She says, "I love having people over on Christmas Eve, including my family, friends, my ex-husband, and his girlfriend. I hold Easter egg hunts for the four grandchildren in my backyard."

Her face is most animated when she speaks of her grandchildren. She sees the two who live in Florida whenever possible. She is called "Ghee," a loving mispronunciation of "Grandma" that actually means "sweet butter" in India. Her daughter Deborah recently confided in Dianne's brother that her mother is "magic" with the children.

Dianne reinvented herself in retirement with a new life in California, where her tireless volunteer efforts help others change

PATRICIA PETERS MARTIN & HELENE DE MONTREUX HOUSTON

their lives. When asked about the biggest surprise of her retirement, something she never expected, Dianne said: "The genuine love and affection from my grandchildren."

Are you surprised?

I hope Dianne's story of resiliency, careful planning, creativity, and courage will inspire you to boldly make the changes your retirement may require. Don't be afraid to try something new!

The Widow Waits to Retire

Mary Ann Igoe
(Patricia)

> *"That I shall love always –*
> *I argue thee*
> *That love is life –*
> *And life hath immortality"*
> *—Emily Dickinson*

Mary Ann Igoe was 66 when her husband of forty-two years died after a short illness. This conscientious master's level nurse practitioner felt helpless watching her husband die within weeks of a metastatic biliary cancer diagnosis. Losing her beloved partner with so little warning brought intense grieving and sorrow.

"I felt completely unprepared and devastated when Bill died. I even questioned whether I wanted to continue my life without him," Mary Ann says.

Her grieving was so intense that she sought counseling with me to help her work through the loss.

Upon meeting Mary Ann in therapy, I couldn't picture her falling apart. She dressed meticulously and even her choice of words seemed measured and guarded. She appeared to "have it all together," yet I knew she felt things were spinning out of control.

Mary Ann had planned carefully all her life, and Bill's untimely death wasn't "in the plan." As a nurse and a wife she grieved not only for her loss, but also because she couldn't help him and somehow change the outcome.

Mary Ann came from a family of four and grew up in Worcester, Massachusetts. Her father, an electrical engineer, retired at the age of 62 with his pension from the power company; seven years later Mary Ann's mother died of cancer. Her father remarried twice more and buried the next two wives. He lived in a retirement home in a neighboring town from Mary Ann and recently died at 102. He always said that he retired too early—what an understatement! Forty years retired and still getting his pension. Perhaps his early retirement comments influenced Mary Ann's later decisions.

When Mary Ann met Bill on a blind date, he was a school teacher and she worked as a pediatric nurse. That single date turned out to be love at first sight, with each of them telling their friends they knew they were going to marry each other that first night. They went on to have two children and enjoy a beautiful, loving marriage for forty-two years, but it ended far too soon with Bill just 73 and Mary Ann 66.

Bill had retired from teaching at age 64, but continued working part time for a neighbor, while Mary Ann continued working as a nurse in a private medical practice. They saved well for retirement, but Mary Ann wasn't ready to leave her profession. In fact she had gone back to school for a Bachelor's degree in nursing and then earned an advanced degree as a nurse practitioner while raising their two children. Some of Mary Ann's instructors were less than supportive because of her age, and she wondered, "Why am I doing this at my age?"

But Bill—always her cheerleader when things got tough—said, "Of course, you'll be able to do it, and you'll be great."

"That was just like him, to always support me," she says. After his death Mary Ann was glad she had the foresight to attend school during those years, because working as a nurse practitioner helped her survive Bill's death. "We made such a great team! That's why it's so hard to be without him now," she reminded me.

Left alone after Bill died, Mary Ann found comfort in the structure and stimulation of her work. She is a caring and conscientious nurse practitioner—exactly the kind of person you'd want to care for you or a loved one.

"I kept wondering when I'd feel the urge to retire," Mary Ann says. As her 70's approached she cut back to three days a week, then in her seventies she worked only two and a half days. All these years she continued reading medical journals, attending seminars, and staying involved with healthcare changes. No one wanted her to leave, but at 73 years of age, Mary Ann decided the time had come. She told me, "I worried a lot about making mistakes. It hadn't happened yet, but the stress of worrying began to wear me down."

The office staff and patients were sorry to lose her, but Mary Ann just *knew*. "I guess I got my money's worth out of my extra education. I worked twenty more years!"

"What was your biggest concern about leaving?" I asked her.

"I was afraid of feeling bored and lonely," she responded. "I knew I'd be okay financially, so I took the leap."

"And how did that work out?"

Well, my worries were ridiculous because I love retirement. I got a bicycle at age 73 and love riding around the neighborhood and with my grandsons. My eyesight isn't the best, but I don't let that hold me back.

"I also enjoy not having to say, 'I can't do that. I have to work.' Plus, I don't have constant worry and reminders about how my patients are doing. I'm surprised that I don't miss working. I thought I'd be sad—but I'm NOT."

"Did anything in particular make retiring easier for you?" I asked.

"I think gradually cutting my hours from five, to four, to three, and then two days a week helped a lot with the transition. I eased out the door a little at a time—and the office got used to functioning without me. I waited and listened to myself. When the time came I knew it was right."

"What's the hardest thing about retirement?" I asked.

"Being alone is still a challenge for me at times," she said. "After all those wonderful years with Bill, I still miss his companionship. But I found ways to cope with every issue that came up." Here's Mary Ann's list of things that bring joy to her life:

- Family
- Friends
- Exercise
- Lifelong learning
- Church
- Travel

Mary Ann is fortunate to live near her children and their families. She is a wonderful example of a holistically well person: she exercises, cares for her health, does Tai Chi, yoga and Pilates, and is involved socially with lots of friends. She takes lifelong learning courses and has an active spiritual life with her church.

Because Mary Ann is a planner, she made certain to arrange things she could look forward to. Before leaving her job she'd already planned a course she wanted to take and a trip to Africa. "Everyone needs things to look forward to," she says. "Even if it's just taking a walk or having a nice meal, we should plan events that bring joy into our lives."

Mary Ann has followed the advice of Dan Buettner, author of *The Blue Zones (2010)* whose research suggests a long, productive life is associated with putting family ahead of other concerns and being socially active and integrated into your community.

Other advice from Mary Ann includes:

Don't retire until you feel ready. You'll know when the time comes.

Start planning early for things you'll do in retirement. Make a special effort to fill your life with things you'll enjoy. This is your special time of life.

Stay active socially and keep yourself physically fit. Even if you have health problems, take good care of yourself and push yourself to be active.

"I never thought I'd be alone in retirement. Keep that in mind while you're planning. You could be with a partner; you might be someone's caregiver; or you may end up living on your own. No matter what, you can still enjoy life, contribute to the community, and keep growing."

Bill has been gone for six years and Mary Ann still misses him daily. But she hopes to find companionship again and looks forward to travelling while she's physically fit. After the trip to Africa, she's planning excursions to Asia and South America.

Mary Ann's strength, determination, and exploration of new things and people gives hope to everyone who becomes a widow or widower.

NOTES

Dan Buettner, *The Blue Zones: Lessons for Living Longer from the People Who've Lived Longest,* Washington, D.C., The National Geographic Society, 2010.

Mary Ann and Bill Igoe

From Consciousness Raising to Lifelong Learning

Janet and Paul Wolvek

(Helene)

"I am still learning." Michelangelo

Mutual love for music and theater helped draw Janet and Paul Wolvek together. Both were divorced and Janet had two sons when they married in 1990. Janet is a lifelong professional musician who, for many years, was the "go to" piano teacher in their community with at least 35 students at a time.

Paul was a corporate trader and accountant in Manhattan, but his avocation and true love always followed the arts. When he was younger Paul auditioned for plays and musicals at community theaters, which is where he met Janet through her son Jeremy, who performed with him in *Oliver*. Their work together on stage developed into friendship, closeness to the family, and then much more.

Janet says, "I always loved watching Paul perform and he often had leading roles. He starred in *The Nerd, The Mousetrap, The Foreigner, and Barefoot in the Park*." Still proud of his time on the stage, Paul was delighted when Jeremy gained admission to NYU Tisch School of the Arts to major in drama.

Janet and Paul loved attending Broadway shows and Lincoln Center for opera, ballet, and the Philharmonic Orchestra. They also enjoyed world travel, from sunshine in Jamaica to theater tours in London, to Eastern Europe and Russia where they investigated Paul's ancestry.

Their time together might be described as idyllic, but no one has a perfect life. For Paul and Janet, medical crises often brought complications. Paul's health remained good aside from a knee replacement, broken ribs and heart issues, but Janet has had a 40 year struggle with kidney disease that culminated in a kidney transplant 22 years ago. Her kidney outlived most transplants but finally gave up last year. Janet is now on home dialysis. After a harrowing year of life-threatening health scares, her health is currently stable.

"How did you get through all this and manage to stay so upbeat and active?" I asked Janet.

"I had a wonderful husband, as you know, and the other big factor is my forty year membership in special women's group. It started when I moved to a new area with my first husband and was invited by a friend to join a consciousness raising group."

"Exactly what was a consciousness raising group?" I asked.

"These groups started in the late 1960s when feminists wanted to organize, educate women, and increase our awareness of oppression."

"It sounds radical!"

She smiled. Not so radical now, but it was then. Before the 1960s, women were supposed to hold things in and not discuss our feelings or troubles in 'polite society.' In this group I found my voice—as did many other women of my generation.

"Our group evolved beyond the original purpose. At first we followed the topics and guidelines, but it soon turned into a group of close, supportive friends sharing personal struggles and joys. I loved the support I received for parenting, marriage issues, and my serious medical problems."

Janet's friends rallied around her during the year when she was near death on several occasions. "They took turns bringing meals to Paul. He and I were so grateful for their kindness and support."

Janet chose to have home dialysis when she found the three-day a week regimen at the dialysis center exhausting and constraining. "I wasn't able to do the things I love."

Janet adores her older son's child, Henry, who lives in New Jersey. With home dialysis she's more able to take day trips into the city and see plays or visit Henry. She developed a routine system for setting up the machine before going to bed at night. The tubes and noises don't bother her, and she sleeps well. When she awakens the treatment is over and she's free to go about her day.

"I feel so much stronger now. It was a struggle attending my younger son's wedding last fall because I hadn't started dialysis and felt terrible. But now my energy is better and I can enjoy visits with Henry, who never stops moving."

Like many of us, Paul and Janet were able to more fully expand their passions during retirement. Although long distance travel is no longer an option, a shared enthusiasm for art, music, theater, and lifelong learning keeps them busy.

Being self-employed as a piano teacher, Janet could adjust her schedule according to her health needs over the years. Despite the recent health setback she remains committed to teaching her five piano students. "Teaching piano is part of my identity," she says, "and I would hate to give it up. Helping my students improve and excel is a huge part of who I am."

Paul retired from the business world at age 63 and almost immediately picked up painting, something he enjoyed years earlier. To hone his skills and make contacts, he audited community college art classes. He attends every class he can find and found teachers he admires and learns from. He loves doing landscapes and developed a special talent for drawing pet dogs. "Friends from all over the country send me photos and ask if I'll paint their dogs. That's something I like to do for people."

About ten years ago Janet and Paul began taking courses at Mount Saint Mary College Desmond Campus for Adults. Like other programs across the country, the college offers noncredit, life-enriching education for adult learners. In a relaxed atmosphere without the pressure of exams and grades, such courses strike a balance between the practical and the cultural aspects of learning. Their L.I.F.E. program targets adults over 55 and hosts the Road Scholars program on campus every summer. "We take every course we can. They're so stimulating and we feel like we're learning all the time.

"We also met new friends through the classes," Janet says. "A few years ago we took a wonderful seven-week poetry class. The course was so amazing we couldn't bear to see it end. So a group of us—Paul and I, two retired psychologists, and the retired English teacher who led the class—are still meeting."

Janet and Paul graciously hosted a book discussion for me at their new home in Monroe, NY, after *The Other Couch: Discovering Women's Wisdom in Therapy* was published. Their beautiful large living room exploded with friends from her consciousness raising group, adult learning classes, Janet's book group, and her knitting group. This cordial, lively and intellectual group overflowed with life experience and camaraderie.

Later I asked Janet, "What advice do you have for people as they approach retirement?"

She thought for a moment, then said, "To sum it up, I believe everyone needs to look forward to something every day. And we're responsible for making that happen instead of waiting for happiness to come and find us. It's wise to explore things we love to do and find new ways to fit them into our lives, even if we're stuck at home. We find that classes and activities related to the arts are life-affirming and a wonderful distraction from the not so pleasant aspects of life!"

Recent studies show that people live longer when they have social integration (frequent daily interaction with others) and close relationships—people they can count on. By the looks of it, Janet and Paul should be with us for a long, long time.1

The Wolveks and their grandson Henry, who is also Helene's grandson.

NOTES

Julianne Holt-Lunstad, Ph.D. of Brigham Young University has been researching loneliness, social isolation and their relationships to health and longevity. Recent studies reveal that of all the predictors of longevity we know, social integration (frequent daily interactions with many people) and close relationships (people we can count on) are the greatest predictors of long life.

Almost every community has options for lifelong learning, either at nearby colleges or through local groups and clubs. Retirees not only take these classes, but often develop their own courses and teach them. The easiest way to find classes is an internet search under: "lifelong learning classes near me."

Here are a few examples:

The Road Scholar Institute

Founded in 1962 by a group of retired educators, Road Scholars offers fun and stimulating learning adventures to lifelong learners. They are solo travelers, couples, partners, or friends. They are retirees and busy professionals. They are farmers and urbanites, intellectuals, and adventurers. Together, they form a dynamic cohort that enriches every learning experience. The group was formerly called Elderhostel. www.roadscholar.org

Institute for Retired Professionals

Developed by The New School in NYC, this lifelong learning school is located in New York City's Greenwich Village. It is open to retired or semiretired people in their fifties onward who want to actively participate in cooperative learning and instruction.

People of all backgrounds pursue serious, peer-led inquiry through the lifelong learning program. The IRP encourages individuals to challenge themselves by taking part in study groups and assuming academic and administrative leadership roles. Each person's learning experience is enriched through regular exchanges with enthusiastic learners with diverse backgrounds and interests. https://www.newschool.edu/institute-for-retired-professionals/

Free Online Learning Classes

Stan Peirce had been looking for new pursuits after a long career as an electrical engineer. While searching the Internet, he stumbled on nearly 2,000 academic courses the Massachusetts Institute of Technology had put online. Peirce saw MIT's offerings—its OpenCourseWare project complete with syllabuses, assignments, exams and, in many cases, audio or video lectures—as nothing short of an educational gold mine.

"I couldn't believe all of this was available—for free," he says.

Welcome to "e-Learning." Curious about world history or quantum physics? Want to stretch your mind by learning to speak a new language or to play the accordion? Need to fix a leaky faucet or teach your dog to behave? Now you can learn just about anything you want to learn without setting foot in a classroom.

The American Association of Retired Persons (AARP) website, the source of Stan Peirce's story, offers a portal to hundreds of free learning opportunities, plus advice on how to use the programs. (https://www.aarp.org/personal-growth/life-long-learning/info-01-2011/free_online_learning.html)

Open Culture

This website scours the internet for the best free cultural and educational media, including audio books, online courses, great lectures, movies, and ebooks. http://www.openculture.com/

The Company Man and Mandatory Retirement

Edward Machir

(Patricia)

"Don't simply retire from something; have something to retire to." Harry Emerson Fosdick

Ed is a fellow Georgetown Hoya who always sits next to me at our Georgetown University board meetings. When I met Ed, an accountant, he was a partner at PricewaterhouseCoopers (PwC) and living in the Georgetown section of Washington, D.C.

I became fond of Ed's sense of humor, booming voice, and generous spirit. When my youngest daughter Madeleine applied for an internship at PwC, Ed acted as a mentor. Over the years I learned that as a PwC partner Ed would face mandatory retirement at age 60. That seemed young to me, and I wondered how he would handle the situation.

When he learned about this book, Ed praised the help he got from PwC, both financial and emotional, during his transition to retirement.

"Wow!" I said. "You mean this huge corporation actually helps employees get ready for retirement?!"

Even better, PricewaterhouseCoopers gave us permission to discuss their retirement coaching and Ed agreed to tell me how he's handling retirement, now five years out.

Ed was the second son of southern parents who met in D.C. when in their 20's. They found jobs and each other. His father worked in real estate development in the D.C. area. After prep school, Ed was delighted to be accepted by Georgetown, where he found a niche in accounting. His academic career skyrocketed under the mentorship of Professor George Houston. He had discovered aptitude and passion in life.

Ed tells me, "I joined PwC in 1978 and stayed with them for 36 years. For the last 27 years I was a partner.

"While I always knew a transfer from D.C. was possible, reality set in when I was "up for" partner and they wanted to send me to Texas. Fortunately my wife and three kids were incredibly supportive.

"When I look back on that transfer I'm glad it happened, because I was able to grow and take on challenges at a rapid pace—things I couldn't have done in D.C. My career took off in Texas. The savings and loan crisis of the early to mid-1980s gave me an incredible challenge as a young partner. I worked extensively for Bank of America, the FDIC, and the RTC. Showing my ability in different facets of our practice led to bigger and better things."

Ed developed a reputation for handling messy situations. "If it's an ugly job, give it to Machir, and he'll figure how to clean it up," people said. Ed loved his career.

His own life turned messy as the children began leaving the nest and his wife of 26 years asked for a divorce. This blind-sided Ed. They tried counseling, but it wasn't successful. The divorce stung—he felt devastated, but he says, "I just had to gut through it. I knew I had a lot of positive things to help me. I had four great kids and they were still in my life.

"My ex-wife and I tried hard to keep the kids out of the divorce; and as a result we all get along pretty well. We even vacation together with the kids and grandchildren."

Ed still grieves what could have been, but his positive attitude helps him carry on and maintain wonderful relationships with all his children and grandchildren. He realized that while his career was taking off, he and his wife neglected their relationship. In hindsight, he accepts responsibility for this.

Ed's career continued on track and, by 2011 he needed to think about winding down work and "riding off into the sunset." PricewaterhouseCoopers helped with this phase.

Ed says, I may be prejudiced, but PwC always puts people first; those of us at the firm and our clients. Early in my career they advised me about financial retirement. They even ran a program for partners and spouses to discuss the emotional side of retirement.

"I was the first single person to attend this couples' seminar—a two day, off site program run by outside professionals."

"How did they help you think ahead?" I asked.

"For one thing, we discussed how we'd use our time when we stopped showing up at the office every day."

Thinking like a psychologist, I asked, "What about the emotional side of retirement?"

We talked about changes to relationships and they encouraged everyone to share fears, ideas, and concerns with the group to get feedback. We had some great discussions, and plenty of laughter.

"They didn't give us answers—they showed us how to ask the right questions and deal with what's next?'"

Ed remembers the spouses saying, "Is my husband going to hang around the house and expect me to fix his lunch every day? I already have a life."

For better or worse; but not for lunch. That's a quote I've heard about a husband's retirement from stay-at-home women. However, Ed was still single and had no such worries.

First he took a month off at a beach to decompress. By August he was ready to work again. He began teaching a few accounting and auditing courses at the McDonough School of Business at Georgetown University. This gave him time to golf, serve on boards, and serve as chairman of the Georgetown Alumni Admissions

Association. In this capacity he raised over one million dollars for the Georgetown Scholarship Program.

Still relatively young and always a leader, Ed continues doing good work in retirement. He believes his Georgetown education with its motto of "Men and Women for Others" has always guided his career and extracurricular activities.

He says, "I'll keep teaching and volunteering as long as I love what I'm doing. In retirement I get to choose exactly what I want to do. If it gets boring, I change my activity."

He continues, "Now I have a chance to teach and help others with the skills I developed during my career. Mostly it's lots of fun. I'm surprised by how happy I am in retirement."

"Why is that, exactly?" I asked.

He thought for a moment, then said, "I've always loved my work, so I simply carried on with it. But I get to be active with my children and grandchildren, more involved at my country club, and even stay involved with PwC's recruiting and mentoring. What could be better?"

"Were there any surprises?"

I did discover that, even in retirement, I need to move from job to job to keep myself energized and interested. Continuous learning motivates me; I like new challenges and meeting different people. I don't seem to be bored too often.

Also, my struggles with weight didn't automatically disappear with retirement. Over the years I've lost and gained hundreds of pounds. I realized that obesity would ultimately kill me. If I wanted to enjoy my children, grandchildren, and retirement, I needed to LIVE.

"Before retirement I tried a lap-band procedure, but it became infected and didn't work for me. A year ago I put weight loss at the top of my agenda and had a stomach stapling procedure."

"How did that work for you?" I asked.

"Life is better. I lost nearly a hundred pounds and I exercise a lot. I have more energy. I enjoy physical things more. Stretching, working on my balance and core are important if I want to enjoy an active lifestyle, feel younger, and extend my life. I still fight my addiction to sugars, but this is a work in progress and a battle I intend to win."

"Do you enjoy being single?"

He smiles ruefully. "Not so much. I get tired of doing everything by myself and I'd love to find another life partner. I'm afraid I'll feel lonelier as I get older. One of these days I might venture into the dating world, but that's a big step for me."

"And what advice would you give other retirees?"

Don't worry that your life will go from 70 mph to 0 mph. With careful thought and planning you can adjust life to whatever mph you want.

Start preparing early by considering what's important to you. Do you want to give back to others? If so, think about how you'll do it. Visualize how you'll spend time with people you care about and what you can do to stay physically, and mentally, active.

"Retirement is the next step in life, a normal step . . . like going to college, finding a partner, having a child, or changing jobs. We all expect to deal with it. Retirement is a normal transition of life. The thing is—we need to be in charge of our own happiness by planning ahead and taking advantage of all the good things life has to offer."

I'm sure Ed's commitment to physical fitness and serving others, his love of family, his sense of humor, and his infectious personality will continue helping him create a fulfilling, successful retirement.

NOTES

Ed's concern with his weight is reinforced by the research of Roger Landry, M.D., in his book *Live Long, Die Short*. He states that "obesity is associated with multiple serious threats to our health, independence, and even our very lives."

You will find further information on healthy eating for older adults at www.choosemyplate.gov. MyPlate for Older Adults focuses on the unique nutritional and physical-activity needs associated with aging and is intended to be a guide for healthy older adults.

Roger Landry, M.D., MPH, *Live Long, Die Short*, Greenleaf Book Group Press, Austin, Texas, 2014. (page 130).

Emotional Wellness

My Day, My Way: My Fourth Quarter of Life

Carol Kane

(Patricia)

"Age is an issue of mind over matter. If you don't mind, it doesn't matter." Mark Twain

I met Carol shortly after her 101 year old mother died, when Carol herself was 78 years old. Carol suffered from insomnia and anxiety after her mother passed away within a year of her younger sister's death at 67. Now facing the fourth quarter century of her life, Carol decided to pause and reevaluate her next steps.

I visited Carol's loft style condominium on a beautiful autumn day for our book interview. An attractive, engaging woman, Carol doesn't look or act 78 years old. Her upbeat attitude, clothing, and decorating style indicate she keeps up with things. Seated in her comfortable living room, we started by talking about Carol's early life.

In the 1950s when she grew up, most women's career choices were limited to nursing, teaching, or secretarial work. Her dream of being a pharmacist wasn't an option, so Carol enrolled in nursing school at age 16.

By age 18, Carol was engaged to be married. She explains, "The expected future and goal in those days was to marry and have a family. I was impatient to get on with life! And with all the wisdom of my 18 years, the ever present A-bomb threat, and no "career opportunity" expectations to aim for, I left nursing school, got married, and had four children—two boys and two girls. My husband became an executive in the computer industry. This occupation required many transfers—we moved twelve times in twenty years. Those were adventurous times. When the children reached middle school/high school age we put down roots in California."

When Carol's youngest child started nursery school she remembers sitting at the kitchen table drinking her morning coffee after everyone else left. A neighbor woman drove by on her way to college classes, looking happy and fulfilled.

Carol told herself, "In one or two years you can be sitting here with a cup of coffee—or with a diploma."

Carol decided she wanted that diploma, so she attended the local community college part time for four years to become a registered nurse. She worked the night shift at a local hospital while the children were in school. She loved it.

"I needed to work for my sense of self-esteem," she said. "You don't get a medal for raising kids, so I needed something more to fulfill me and give me a sense of identity."

As the children entered college and left the nest, Carol stretched her intellectual curiosity by working as a nurse in research projects at Stanford University. When one grant ended, Carol would find work in another area of research. One of her favorite jobs was working for a female medical doctor doing research on AIDS in the early 1990s.

Around this time, Carol's husband began taking leaves of absence from work for up to three months, during which he would travel and enjoy himself. Carol went with him on these adventures, but she soon realized her husband was having some kind of mid-life crisis.

After 30 years of marriage he came home one day and said, "I want to move out and live apart." He didn't ask for a divorce; he just wanted to separate. He continued paying the bills and started to work on boats and sail and do "his own thing."

Carol says, "I literally saw my life pass before my eyes when he told me he wanted to separate. I was heartbroken. It took a good three years being separated before I finally filed for divorce. I was 48 years of age when he dropped the separation bomb on me, and 52 when I became a divorced woman. This was never something I planned on or saw coming, but I had to adapt."

Carol was able to downsize and sell the family home. She began working in the field of AIDS research conducting clinical trials, and stayed in this position for ten years, happy to have an interesting job and great colleagues.

At age 62, Carol decided to retire. She and her husband had never talked about retirement, just as they never talked about divorce. Laughing, Carol said, "We were going along fat, dumb, and healthy, and just never thought about retirement." At 62 she collected her Social Security, took the money from her California home sale, and moved back to Western Massachusetts where her mother, sister, and brother lived.

Like many people her age, Carol realized she wasn't ready to actually stop working. It took her about a year to find the perfect job, another research position in Western Massachusetts at a satellite office for Boston AIDS research. Back in her element, she loved her job and worked several days a week from age 63 to 72 years of age. She didn't need the money, but she liked the work and her colleagues. She needed to feel connected.

By 2010, AIDS research was winding down and Carol felt, "people deserve my best, and as I aged I felt it was time to let my nursing license expire."

She saw this as phasing out; not a retirement.

Carol was free to travel with her mom and sister. She bought a summer trailer at the Rhode Island shore, played Mahjong, and enjoyed life. Carol felt this was her time to explore and enjoy special things. She tried new ventures, but if she didn't enjoy something she had no trouble saying, "This is not for me."

"I found so many things to do and try for the first time!" she added.

After her mother and sister passed away, Carol evaluated whether to stay in Massachusetts or move closer to her children out West. She had many friends in New England and enjoyed the four seasons. She had to think. Carol says, "My life wasn't really planned as much as it evolved. This was the next evolution. I decided to stay in New England and visit my children and grandchildren rather than live next door to them. That has worked for me so far."

When asked about retirement, Carol looked puzzled. "I don't feel retired. I'm still learning every day. You know you can learn a lot if you watch the right television shows!"

Carol loves to scrapbook and make lovely greeting cards for all occasions. She says, "I enjoy my own company and doing things I like. Sometimes, I want to stay in all day; other days I get out and socialize. If I stay in the house too many days in a row I begin feeling isolated and unloved. Then I know it's time to get out and socialize." She jokingly says, "I go to Whole Foods, fondle the asparagus, wonder where it came from, and feel connected again!"

When I asked about purpose and "mattering" in life, Carol had a quick retort. "I don't want to matter anymore! I've mattered to others all my life. And though it might sound selfish, this is now "MY DAY, MY WAY!"

I don't want any more obligations as a nurse or caretaker. However, that doesn't mean I won't do things for others—it's just that it will be my choice about when and how I matter.

And I do want to be remembered by and matter to my twelve grandchildren. So I'm planning to take each of them on a trip..... if I live that long. I've already been on a back-packing trip, gone to Scotland and England and stayed in inexpensive bed and breakfasts, and gone to my trailer for a beach week. That's four grandchildren down, eight more trips to go. If I live long enough maybe I'll get to take my eight great grandchildren on a trip.

"I'm leaving on a train next week to visit my daughter and son and grandchildren in California. I love buying a one way ticket. No need to plan further, I just let the weeks evolve, and come back when I want."

This is truly living my day, my way!

Carol says, Retirement is taking the time for a new look at old habits—your hair, your clothes, travel, health, food, friends, and family.

"I advise everyone push through an uncomfortable situation once—try different things; if you don't like something you can say, 'This is not for me.' But don't hesitate to try things!"

Carol also suggests everyone should save and manage money to have enough freedom to do things in the future.

"My wish for the future is to spend more time with my grand- and great-grandchildren, but the challenge is to find that time due to distance and commitment logistics. My grandchildren and great grandchildren are so special. I call them my fourth quarter reward! I love the time we share, the conversations we have. I feel smarter every time I say goodbye."

She goes on to say "I wonder what I can give and share with them to enrich their futures, and I don't mean just monetarily. I often ponder what knowing about your grandparents really means? What life lessons do I want to share?"

Carol Kane

As I leave Carol's home I notice a plaque on the wall that says, "Today is a good day for a good day." With that kind of attitude and her sense of humor, Carol is bound to have a full and satisfying next twenty years.

NOTES

Generativity

The need Carol feels to share her knowledge is referred to in Erik Erikson's final book, *Vital Involvement in Old Age*. Erikson discusses 8 stages of life and refers to the concept of *generativity*, which mean "making your mark" on the world by creating or nurturing things that will outlast you. The opposite of generativity is stagnation. Erikson identifies later-in-life generativity as "to incorporate care for the present with concern for the future, for today's younger generations and their futures, for generations not yet born, and for the survival of the world as a whole."

Achieving wisdom and sharing it with others is indeed a noble goal for retirement!

Erik Erikson, Joan Erikson, and Helen Kivnich, *Vital Involvement in Old Age*, (New York: Norton, 1986).

Converting Grief Into a Memorial: A Couple's Love Story

Rhonda and Carl Steeg

(Helene)

> *"Philanthropy and social change work are at their best when*
> *they are driven by your values and connected to what you*
> *care about most." Charles Bronfman*

Rhonda and Carl have shared a love story for the ages. Carl is seventeen years her senior and they've been married for 36 years, both for the second time.

Rhonda is an attractive, petite woman who seems ageless and retains the incandescent beauty of her youth. Her love story with Carl began during the illness of her only child Greg at Columbia Presbyterian Medical Center. Not quite three years old, Greg suffered from an astrocytoma, a large tumor in his brain that created a seizure disorder. Rhonda and her husband were separated, but remained attentive and distraught parents to Greg, who was full of personality and adorably cute.

Carl, who was Greg's pediatric cardiologist, appeared at the doorway in a white coat and introduced himself. A strong, imposing man, Carl's serious and thoughtful demeanor masked his humor, intelligence, and huge heart.

Rhonda says, "I'll never forget the moment I first saw Carl in the doorway. I was scared to death, but his calm bedside manner inspired all of us with confidence and hope for Greg."

Carl adds, "I was smitten with Rhonda the moment we met. My wife and I were separating, but I couldn't pursue a relationship with Rhonda until Greg was no long under my care. That gave me extra incentive to help him get better!"

Greg did survive his health problems and Rhonda married Carl when Greg was nine years old. During the ceremony Greg acted as Carl's best man and conscientiously guarded the wedding rings.

Greg's illness led to lifelong health challenges. When Greg was three years old and just beginning treatment, Rhonda asked the surgeon, "How should I treat him?"

The doctor responded, "Treat him every day as though he'll live to be 110 years old." And they did just that. For 30 years Rhonda, Carl, and Greg's father worked as a team to keep Greg safe, happy, and productive. They all wanted him to have the most normal life possible. In 2011, Greg's condition worsened and he passed away. During the final weeks he chose to visit his father in California and that home became his hospice. Before his passing Greg loved hearing stories from his case manager, Isa (with Jewish Family and Children's Services in Boston) about Isa's home in Africa and his work there with children who had so little. Greg's last act was to buy buckets of candy for Isa to take to those children.

During those years Carl and Rhonda's professional lives flourished as Carl continued practicing pediatric cardiology and Rhonda enjoyed her human resources career. Carl retired at age 65 to pursue his retirement goal of volunteering for the arts.

He says, "I happily became a docent for the NY Library of the Performing Arts Jerome Robbins Dance Division and for the New York City Ballet. I also volunteered as a tour guide for Lincoln Center and as an ESL teacher.

I always loved the arts, especially dance. Perhaps in another life I would have pursued it myself. Retiring from medicine allowed me to fulfill the dreams I had to put aside.

"I also dreamed up a new medical consultation business called It's Like Having a Doctor in the Family, where I could translate what people's doctors were telling them into plain English.

Unfortunately, the business never really took off. That was my only real disappointment in retirement," he says.

Twenty years later Carl's health remains good, although he recently had a knee replacement and cut back on his volunteer work. Although he appreciated the freedom from his medical schedule in his retirement, paradoxically he sometimes misses having a routine.

Rhonda, now 63, retired four years ago. From a coworker friend who also married a man many years her senior, she learned to plan for and appreciate the years she and Carl could share. Her friend delayed retirement and her husband passed away before they could enjoy it together. Rhonda didn't let that happen.

Carl and Rhonda enjoy traveling and attending theatrical and dance performances together. They are much involved with their complex, blended family where events often include all the "exes" and step children. Greg loved each and every member of the family and they still feel his love. Despite all his challenges he loved to say, "I am so lucky."

Rhonda serves on a theater board of directors, which keeps them both involved in the arts. Rhonda admits she often feels pressed for time because she tends to overcommit and has difficulty saying no.

"There's so much I want to do. When I retired I thought I'd have all the time in the world, but I don't. I still have an overscheduled life."

"How do you view your retirement?" I asked Carl.

"Among other things, it's a time to reflect back on life and connect with the good I did and the people I helped."

Rhonda adds, "People shouldn't worry about having nothing to do. I think retirement is a time for giving back, donating money or time, and doing something different."

Regarding Greg, both Carl and Rhonda can look back with pride on how they helped him lead a full life and accomplish many things in spite of overwhelming health challenges. They often think about how Greg's generous spirit touched their lives and many other lives. Two years ago Greg's beloved caseworker Isa contacted them about a school he was developing in the village of Shabwafwa, Zambia for poor children. He wanted to name the school in Greg's memory and asked if they would help with fundraising.

Rhonda says, "The school, The Mwashinyambu Greg Baker Community School, was dedicated in 2016. The children and community celebrate Greg's birthday every year, and we're always there to share in the celebration and love." Isa Ebowe, now president of Generis International, states he built the school in Greg's honor. "His selfless nature will help give orphans and underprivileged children the opportunity for education that will last a lifetime."

The Steegs at Greg Baker School in Zambia

"The school has changed our lives," Carl added. "Now we often say, 'We are so lucky,'" just as Greg used to.

The story of Rhonda, Carl, and Greg contains several inspiring facets: how the power of love can bring people together and effect social change; the possibility for couples to be close and yet pursue different interests; and the challenges of marriage with significant age differences.

Rhonda and Carl present a fine example of the need for flexibility and adjustment when dealing with retirement. Thank you so much for sharing your special story of love.

Greg Baker (Steeg) Bar Mitzvah

I Feel Like Myself Again

Jane Doe

(Patricia)

"There is a vitality, a life force, an energy, a quickening translated through you into action, and because there is only one of you in all time, this expression is unique. And if you block it, it will never exist through any other medium and will be lost." Martha Graham

All I Have is All I Need.

I came to know Jane Doe when her divorce attorney recommended she see me for therapy. During that time, Jane—who uses this name to protect herself and her children—was in the middle of a chaotic, emotionally abusive marriage, trying to make heads or tails of the situation. A year or so later a judge granted her a divorce on the grounds of cruel and abusive treatment.

Fast forward many years and Jane's life has dramatically changed. She says, "I feel like myself again. I live on a budget these days, but my limited choices make the things I have all the more valuable."

Jane's story of courage, resilience, and inspiration is a reminder that each of us can live a better life if we make the courageous, often difficult decision to leave toxic and abusive situations and relationships. Although she suffered traumatic life events, Jane continues helping others with grace and generosity of spirit. Her retirement years, though not as financially secure as she once imagined, turned into a welcome period of joy, simplicity, and authenticity.

Nothing in Jane's childhood predicted the way her life would go off track. Her journey began outside Pittsburgh, Pennsylvania as the fourth daughter of five children, with her only brother coming four years after Jane's birth. Her mother was a stay-at-home mom while raising young children and her Dad worked long hours managing grocery stores.

Jane remembers, "My mom read a lot, and she took all five of us kids to the public library every week. My goal was to read all the books in the grade school section of the library—and I got close! Mom led a Great Books enrichment program at my school and directed one act plays every year for the Catholic Youth Organization. I was proud of her."

After high school Jane's parents separated in what she called a Catholic-style divorce—living apart, but no legal divorce. They remained friendly and attentive to the children while living separate lives. When asked about college Jane reluctantly and humbly says, "I worked hard at school and was awarded a Regent's scholarship to attend Carnegie Mellon tuition free. For financial reasons I had to live home with my mom and I did the cooking and cleaning in lieu of room and board. I continued to waitress at a local restaurant where I'd worked since tenth grade. Somehow I pulled off graduating Phi Beta Kappa and magna cum laude and was awarded grants and loans to study at Boston University Law School. While at law school I only had a bicycle for transportation and I would bike to Harvard Square where I worked as a waitress, go to classes, and do work-study with a law professor. That was a busy but exciting time for me. And I did it! I graduated cum laude from Boston University Law School in three years."

Jane's future looked bright, especially because she also fell in love during law school. John, a fellow law student was handsome, smart, and charming. Jane occasionally saw glimpses of a critical, controlling side to his character, such as telling her how to dress and style her hair. She had limited experience with dating, so she believed the answer was to try harder to please him. Early in their relationship John cheated on Jane and she immediately broke up with him. But John dramatically and profusely apologized, told her how much he loved her, and promised he'd never cheat again. Jane, who is forgiving by nature, was willing to try again.

She remembers, "When I married John after law school we were full of hope. We decided to live in Western Massachusetts where we both found work in law. I honestly thought everything was fine in our marriage for years. We had three children and life was busy, but happy. John often came home late, but I believed this was part of working his way up in the law firm; I viewed his time away as a sacrifice for the family.

"I needed to stop working after we discovered our youngest had severe health issues. Eventually, when my youngest entered school I began teaching at a local high school. I loved this work and was awarded Teacher of the Year several times."

Jane goes on, But, unfortunately, I was fooled by my husband and my world exploded when he came home late one evening and told me I should be tested for gonorrhea. He said it like he was telling me we needed milk from the store. After the few seconds it took to process what he meant, I slid out of my chair and fell to the floor. When I finally managed to ask him 'How did this happen?' He told me he'd been with a prostitute when he went out with a client and got drunk, but it was only one time. Like doing it just once made everything okay.

It was humiliating, but I went to my gynecologist and got tested. I was positive for gonorrhea. My doctor was great and told me I should see a divorce attorney. I made an appointment with an attorney and she said until I got a grip I wouldn't be able to make good decisions through the divorce proceedings. That's when I began counseling with Dr. Martin. And it's a good thing I started therapy because I came to realize over the next few months that my husband had been leading a secret double life with affairs and prostitutes throughout our entire marriage. How devastating it was to realize my whole marriage was a sham! Although it took years, I finally divorced this evil man.

Jane continues, "I lost myself in the marriage, trying too hard and creating constant excuses and adjustments to make things work. The divorce itself was awful, but that ordeal led to a much saner and calmer life. I had to rediscover myself: What I liked doing, what my true interests were, and how I wanted to live my remaining life.

"Shortly after my divorce I was recruited to teach in the social studies program of a different high school. There, I created my own curriculum for a legal studies component. With the joys and challenges of this job I began feeling alive again. Seeing myself valued by the faculty and students made me happy."

Jane glows as she talks about her love of teaching and I can imagine the knowledge those fortunate students gained during her 14 years teaching high school. However, she finally decided to leave the profession.

"I loved teaching, but I just had to retire five years ago because of the crazy new compliance regulations for teachers—especially the outcome measures. I adored my students and would have taught 'til I dropped, but I couldn't take all the meaningless paperwork that pulled energy and time away from actually teaching."

"And how did you envision your retirement?" I asked her.

My image of retirement was from the movie *On Golden Pond*—a cabin on a lake in the woods of Vermont or New Hampshire, with occasional trips into NYC or Boston for culture.

However, I always planned on retiring with my husband and living on our combined savings and pensions. That vision blew up when I discovered his double life and realized I didn't know the man I married.

"I've had to adjust to my new status, but I like being able to adapt and no longer feeling like a leaf blown about by his wind. With family, friends, and therapy, I mostly healed, and now I trust myself a lot more."

Now Jane says she is busier than ever, volunteering in the areas of domestic abuse and human trafficking as well as taking classes at local colleges.

What I like best about retirement is writing, doing advocacy and volunteer work, taking classes, and having occasional lunches and dinners with friends.

"What I like least is worrying the state will bankrupt my pension, Congress will shrink or eliminate Social Security and Medicare, and the stock market will crash. I rely on these three legs as if they were a stool."

When asked what she would change about retirement, Jane says, "Although I sometimes wish I could travel on long adventures, I've come to appreciate and even love what I have: three grown children, a house, a car, a garden, and a library. I have a quote on my desk that says: *All I have is all I need*."

"What advice do you have for others?" I asked Jane.

Young people just starting off on their own should start a pension plan or savings account, even if it is only $25 a month. I know it's hard to think about old age when you're still young, but I wish I'd done more planning.

For people getting reading to retire, I say: It's time to shift your perspective. See your wrinkles as wisdom lines, your sagging body as streamlined, and your aching joints as great reasons to take a morning walk and spend the afternoons reading.

"I have found myself again. The things I struggle with now don't seem important after what I've been through in the past. I love my children and I can make decisions that are good for me and for them. I live on a budget. I can't have everything, but that just makes the things I have all the more precious.

"It's ironic that I now have time to think and reflect and wonder and appreciate, but the years left in my life are shorter. After all I've been through I know in my bones any day could be my last. I just hope it doesn't end until I clean out my attic!"

Pre-retirement: Listen to Your Emotions and Your Body

Sister Ann Marie

(Patricia)

> *"If you consciously let your body take care of you, it will become your greatest ally and trusted partner."*
> Deepak Chopra

> *"Everything you need to know is within you. Listen. Feel. Trust the body's wisdom."*
> Dan Millman

Although many people look forward to retirement, this event can also bring major stress into our lives. We leave the familiar surroundings of friends and colleagues, possibly move to a new home, and often feel emotionally and physically exhausted during the final months of wrapping things up at a job.

Sister Ann Marie is a classic example of learning to listen to your emotions and your body during that pre-retirement year. I met this dynamic nun when she became president of a small liberal arts college in Massachusetts, following a two year sabbatical. Her sabbatical came after spending nineteen years as president of a college in upstate New York.

Fascinated, I watched this 68 year old woman firmly take the helm of an academic ship in financial trouble—a ship that desperately needed ballast and stability. At a time of life when most people would retire and relax, this small, gutsy, white-haired woman took on a major challenge.

She told me, "As sisters, we don't retire. There is always a purpose for us. After leaving the college in New York, I felt too young to retire. After nineteen years as president I had so much to offer."

The stars aligned at the end of her sabbatical, which included a year with her aging mother who would die within a few months. "I began the new presidency six months after my mother's death," Sister Ann Marie says.

For seven years she made significant changes to her new college that included a surge in enrollment, holding a capital campaign for a new science building, improving campus infrastructure, creating valuable links with community colleges, and developing several graduate level degrees.

"I set goals for myself to enhance and strengthen the college. Once we reached those goals I seriously thought about retiring. By then I was 76 years old."

"How did it feel to finally reach that point?" I asked.

"I wondered about many things. What would my identity become when I went from president to ex-president? What about my relationships and friendships—how would they change? How would I find a purpose in life? And on the practical side, where would I live?"

As Sister Ann Marie let go of her career as college president, she also felt the college separating from her. This was disconcerting and a bit frightening. In addition, shortly before retirement she had a cancer scare that required a biopsy. She worried that her plans to live on her own might change if she needed chemotherapy.

For the first time in her life Sister Ann Marie felt tired and weak. Normally a dynamic woman, she felt so overcome by fatigue that she couldn't even pack to move. She told her primary care physician she just wasn't feeling right.

"Are you under stress?" he asked.

Sister Ann Marie said, "Well, yes—I've been under stress for seven years, but now I'm retiring, so shouldn't my stress be going away?"

"Sometimes people feel anxious when they're retiring," the doctor said. This was of little help to Sister Ann Marie. Her condition became so bad that one day she had symptoms of a heart attack and was rushed to the emergency room. The doctor there diagnosed her with panic attacks and emotional exhaustion.

The diagnosis came as a relief and also a revelation. Sister Ann Marie was shocked to learn that she—a woman who served in stressful jobs for over 40 years, was suddenly having anxiety issues. She NEVER had anxiety problems. She was truly surprised and taken unaware by this change in her emotional and physical well-being.

"What do wish you'd known beforehand?" I asked her.

"People need to be aware of the emotional stress they'll go through during the pre-retirement year. This transition can be emotionally and physically draining, and you need to think about how you'll care for yourself. Plan for more rest and give yourself plenty of vacation time during that final year."

She adds, "It's okay to protect your energy, take time off, and think about what you want to do next."

Sister Ann Marie now realizes she had major stress in her life during the final year of work. "Even though you think you're heading into the home stretch and can take it easy at the end, the truth is people may put extra demands on you. You need to be refueling during that last year, not running out of gas.

"Now that I'm retired, it's a breeze. But that final year took a huge toll on me."

Like marriage, children, and the death of our parents, retirement is a major life transition with its own set of stressors. Saying goodbye to familiar routines and colleagues, a new financial status, and losing part of your identity are just a few of the changes.

Like Sister Ann Marie, you may have health issues (her cancer scare, which fortunately turned out to be benign.) All these events combined for Sister Ann Marie to become a perfect storm, causing her body to shut down for a time.

She is now happily settled into an apartment and reconnecting with friends from her former days as college president. But she learned a valuable lesson: We must pay attention to our physical and emotional health.

"If I want to be well, enjoy myself, and continue living alone in this second floor apartment, I need to stay physically well," she says.

A friend suggested and kindly paid for her to see a nutritionist where she was evaluated, went on a three week detox diet, and changed her eating habits. She joined a gym that takes a holistic wellness approach and she walks for an hour every day.

She says, "My body is telling me to slow down—it's time to chill a bit, but also stay healthy and active. I call this my Advent phase, the waiting period, the nurturing time. What will my next period of time evolve to? It will come . . . .but not yet."

NOTES

Sister Sandra Schneiders, a prolific writer, lecturer and consultant, has written many books about women religious. She discusses how religious do not retire, but rather change ministries as they age. She speaks of aging as the 3rd Phase, a time to do things you want to do and to stay active and alive. She says people live too long now to think of retirement at 60 or 70.

As Sandra Schneiders said recently in *Global Sisters Report*, "I don't intend to withdraw from active ministry until I'm unable to be of service . . . Retirement is not quite part of the program for women religious."

The fact that she uses the word "withdraw" is interesting, because the derivation of the word retire from the French retirer, means to withdraw. Do we really want to withdraw from life as we retire? Evidently, that is not part of the mission or plan for women religious.

Jamie Manson, "Biblical scholar Sr. Sandra Schneiders celebrates four milestones," GlobalSistersReport.org., January 25, 2017.

Spiritual Wellness

I Found My New Purpose

Kathleen

(Patricia)

> *"The purpose of life is not to be happy. It is to be useful, to
> be honorable, to be compassionate, to have it make some
> difference that you have lived and lived well."*
> *Ralph Waldo Emerson*

> *"Your purpose in life is to find your purpose and give your
> whole heart and soul to it."*
> *Gautama Buddha*

I met Kathleen at a yoga class when she rolled out her mat next
to mine and we exchanged a friendly greeting. I immediately felt
attracted by her warm, engaging smile and the natural glow of her
beauty. Her sparkly aquamarine eyes invited me to become her
friend, and dimples accompanied her ready laugh and smile. Her

beautiful white hair, cut fashionably just below her ears indicated she might be in her sixties, but on the yoga mat she had the grace of a young woman.

As we became friends over months of shared yoga classes, I realized Kathleen had a spiritual presence far beyond the average person. I wondered if she was retired and how she lived her earlier life. In time, I discovered Kathleen has an amazing story to tell; a story that combines tragedy with the strength, inner wisdom, grace, and peace that is part of a yoga practice.

Kathleen was born into a middle class, Irish immigrant family in Springfield, Massachusetts. "We were poor, but everyone was, so you didn't think of yourself as needy. We lived in public housing until I was 13. Even though my dad had a middle income job, with 11 kids and Mom at home, funds were tight."

Her father worked in middle management at the paper factory and each child was responsible for helping her mother raise this wild brood of children. As the oldest daughter, Kathleen carried much of the burden. She confided to me, "It wasn't long into my life, probably around twelve years of age, when I decided I'd never have children. Been there, done that!"

Kathleen was a so-so student, reading all the time, but not academically motivated. She didn't like to study and as an adult was diagnosed with ADD. After high school she attended a nearby college to become a dental hygienist. She jumped at the chance for more education, seeing this as a way out of responsibilities at home. She enjoyed the social life at school and did well with her studies.

During the last weeks of her first year she met a handsome guy at a fraternity party. Mike was older and more suave than the other frat boys. This attracted her. She soon discovered he was a townie, a local guy who hung out at frat parties to meet college coeds. In no time at all they became a twosome. Mike took her on exciting motorcycle rides around the countryside, gave her beer, and taught her the pleasures of the body. He lavished her with all the attention she'd been denied as a girl from a large family who rarely got individual praise and encouragement.

But his attention soon became overwhelming as he forbade her to associate with other people. She thought this meant he loved her. Soon she began to "play house" with Mike, cooking dinner at his apartment and having a nice table set when he got home from work. He was impressed with her skills in the kitchen and suggested she didn't need to go to school, as he had a nice home right there. Kathleen felt loved in a certain way, but Mike became even more controlling. He told her not to leave the apartment and bolted the door when he left for work so she couldn't get out. He even nailed the windows shut. In these days before cell phones, Mike didn't have a land line phone in his apartment, so Kathleen was a prisoner.

Her friends noticed when she stopped attending classes and they couldn't find her on campus. A group of guys from the fraternity knew she'd been hanging around with Mike and looked for her at his apartment. There they found her, bedraggled, crying, and locked in the bathroom. They rescued her, but it was too late for college because she missed all the final exams. Kathleen left school in disgrace. She felt ashamed, had missed her period, and thought she was pregnant. Returning home pregnant would be unthinkable to her strict Irish Catholic mother and father.

So she boarded a train and ended up in New York City. This lovely, pathetically thin, blond haired innocent was quickly picked up by a "kind" woman she met at the train station. The woman cleaned her up, fed her, and began introducing her to wealthy men. All Kathleen had to do was be "nice" to these men and she would have a safe, warm bed to sleep in. And thus began a two month career as an escort for successful business men.

She escaped the brothel because she needed medical care after contracting a venereal disease. In a high class escort business you don't work when you have a venereal disease. Her period had returned as she put on weight from a healthier diet. Kathleen wanted to go home, so she told her "trainer" she wanted to leave. She was told that wasn't allowed.

Kathleen said, "Then you can tell them I ran away. I'm not getting paid and I don't want to be here anymore."

Kathleen thinks her trainer felt sorry for her and also a bit threatened by Kathleen's intelligence, perhaps concerned Kathleen would move up in the ranks and get her job. So the woman allowed Kathleen to "run away."

Kathleen had called home to let her family know she wasn't dead. She told them her sad story and her father said, "You can always come home."

Back with her family, she fell into the role of mothering the growing children. Again, Kathleen vowed to never have children of her own. Her parents encouraged her to finish the dental hygiene program and she started working in community service dentistry. As soon as she could save enough money she moved into an apartment of her own.

She stayed in touch with her family while making a new life for herself. She married a man she met as a dental patient. John was a handsome guy her age who worked in middle management, like her dad. He was kind, loved her, and treated her well. She says, "I give John credit for building my self-esteem. He often told me how smart I was and I could do anything I put my mind to. He was interested in me as a person, not a sex object."

Early in the relationship Kathleen confided she didn't want children and John agreed. However, he secretly thought she'd change her mind as the marriage progressed. The marriage only lasted six years, because John's suppressed desire to have children grew stronger every year. Kathleen remained adamant on her position and their marriage couldn't survive this difference.

After the divorce, John remarried and became a father within a year. Kathleen moved away and found a dental hygienist job in a thriving dental practice near New York City. She soon began dating an interesting man who agreed with her about children and seemed to be her intellectual match.

"Frank was the love of my life," she says. "We dated for eight years and became a power couple—involved in community activities and always on the go."

Frank frequently travelled on business, but they spent much quality time together. "We were a male/female version of each other in so many ways," Kathleen recalls.

But after eight years of loving partnership, Frank told Kathleen he'd met someone who was "more sophisticated and smarter and will help advance my career." He didn't mention that she also had children and was rich.

This break-up devastated Kathleen. In addition, her father and beloved grandfather died during that year and several tragic accidents occurred in her family. Kathleen says she had her first "nervous breakdown" after the break-up and spent years getting over it.

Kathleen entered her next relationship for financial security. After losing at love so many times, she decided to try being more practical. She married Mark, who appeared to be a successful businessman. Mark was happy Kathleen didn't want her own children and their "business relationship" marriage worked for twenty-five years. They ran a successful business together and travelled all around the world. She became a free spirit, always looking for new adventures. The business continued doing well and the marriage worked as long as money kept flowing to support their jet set lifestyle.

She thought they were financially prepared for an interesting and exciting retirement. Then she learned Mark had been deceiving her for years about money and was ready to file bankruptcy. He morally bankrupted their relationship by lying to her over and over and practicing corrupt business practices. Soon the marriage also went bankrupt. Kathleen and Mark divorced with little money to split between them.

Kathleen learned to synthesize her unique experiences into a spiritual quest for what is truly important in life. "I realized I had to be true to myself and find happiness living within my belief system. All these encounters were part of my journey, and in each of them I find life lessons that were for my good."

Always a survivor, at age 62, Kathleen returned to her skill as a dental hygienist. She rented a small apartment she could afford and happily settled there. For the next five years she lived a simple life, exploring her spirituality with yoga and mindfulness training.

Her warmth quickly attracted friends and she joined a group of wonderful entrepreneurial women with whom she invested her time and talents into community projects. One of these women was a famous psychologist who did spiritual healing seminars. Kathleen was intrigued and began classes and seminars in the spiritual healing world. She felt she'd found her purpose in life with healing touch work and rejoiced in this next chapter of life.

But life had a new twist ahead, just around the corner. Throughout her life Kathleen always remained close with her family. Although she lived away, she often came home for family gatherings. One of

Kathleen's younger sisters was a chronic alcoholic who had a son with alcohol and other drug problems. The son, Joe (her nephew) married at 18 when his girlfriend became pregnant. He was now the father of a 12, 8 and 2 year old, and both he and his wife were heroin addicts. Kathleen and her family tried to be supportive aunts and uncles, but no one could help Joe with his drug problem. After several close calls the inevitable happened and Joe died at thirty from a heroin overdose. The Department of Child and Family Services took the three children from their heroin addicted mother.

As the children's mother (we will call her Meara) moved in and out of rehab, the family services network searched for family members to help the children avoid the foster care system. Everyone in Kathleen's family already had their hands full with their own children. That left Kathleen, age 65—the woman who vowed never to have children.

Her days as a dental hygienist were coming to an end because of wrist tendonitis. She lived a simple, happy life in her world of yoga, meditation, and spiritual healing work. Now a huge decision loomed before her. Taking three abused children into her home was not how she planned to enter retirement.

A wealthy friend of hers suggested she come stay at her condominium in Vermont and enjoy a season of snow skiing. Kathleen felt this was exactly the respite she needed while she came to terms with this next big life decision.

For three months Kathleen led the good life; skiing outside her door every morning, nice naps in the afternoon, concerts and movies, and a glass of wine to end the evening. Life was good. But as the weeks became months, life without purpose felt boring.

"I never planned to retire like other people retire. I never saw myself as not working at something. My grandparents didn't retire and my dad died before retirement age. I think we just repurpose our purpose. And I believe our purpose is directed from a higher up driving force. We just need to listen for it."

Kathleen meditated and prayed on this important life choice. Would she offer to take some or all of the children? One morning she woke up and knew she had to try and help. She contacted social services and learned the two older children could live with her if she moved to Massachusetts where they resided. The two-year-old lived with Kathleen's younger sister Joan.

With her meager savings Kathleen bought a three bedroom house in a good school district in Massachusetts near her nephew's hometown. Twelve year old great nephew, Luke, and eight year old great niece, Mia, were soon on her doorstep. Within a year, three year old Dylan joined his siblings, because Joan couldn't stand watching social services constantly interrupt his life by returning him to Meara, who still used heroin. Each time, Dylan would flip-flop back to his aunt. Joan had enough, and asked Kathleen to take three year old Dylan.

Kathleen agreed, but insisted on backup from her family. And she wanted a court order giving her guardianship of all three children so they wouldn't be subjected to their biological mother's constant whims.

I met Kathleen at yoga class when she was 68. Little did I know this agile, beautiful woman was a single parent to a fifteen year old great nephew, an eleven year old great niece, and a five year old great nephew.

Kathleen's surprise in her retirement years was finding purpose and meaning in her life by parenting these children.

Struggles continue with the court system and the children's mother, who sobers up every few months and wants to regain custody. Kathleen tries to include Meara in the children's lives, but faces criticism and caustic comments from her. Dylan has behavioral problems in his kindergarten class and constantly seeks Kathleen's attention and reassurance that she will always be his Mommy.

"Although I'm not a typical baby nurturer, I am committed to providing these children with a good home," she says.

Kathleen listened to her spiritual calling and will continue following this new purpose. She is an extremely resilient person and mindful that all things change. As Darwin said, "It is not the strongest of the species that survives, nor the most intelligent. It is the one most adaptable to change."

Kathleen continues taking care of herself with yoga, support from family and friends, time-outs for herself, and psychological counseling for everyone. She is going to succeed. Her spiritual wellness is intact; she found her purpose, and this new family will fare well, thanks to Kathleen's love and the secure home base she creates.

We Were Born to Give

Mark and Julie Pohlman

(Helene)

"Philanthropy is commendable, but it must not cause the philanthropist to overlook the circumstances of economic injustice which make philanthropy necessary."
Martin Luther King Jr.

How does a couple develop a lifelong pattern of philanthropy and environmental activism? Mark and Julie Pohlman have been married 54 years. Mark, now 80, retired at age 65 after a distinguished career as an orthopedic surgeon. Julie, age 78, last worked as a visiting nurse. They have always been a striking couple with Scandinavian height and bearing reminiscent of people in Copenhagen. Both have a serious demeanor, but laugh easily, project humility, and clearly love the adventurous life they shared.

Mark and Julie met when Mark was a senior student at the Columbia University College of Physicians and Surgeons. Julie attended Cornell's School of Nursing. One Sunday in May, Mark noticed Julie sitting in front of him in church and proceeded to stalk her as she walked home.

Julie explains: "As I walked through Central Park, he circled around and appeared in front of me acting kind of weird. He abruptly said, 'Hi, I saw you in church.' I ignored him and kept walking."

Mark who was "just coming off a girlfriend" didn't give up easily. He saw her again on another Sunday and asked her on a date.

Julie says "I told him I had to study for finals." She did agree to a walk in the Central Park Zoo where they discovered they had much in common. Both were in the medical field, loved sports, and came from the Midwest.

Ultimately, Julie rearranged her postgrad summer to stay in the city to be near Mark. In the fall she travelled with friends to Europe. Mark had signed up for a tropical medicine rotation in Liberia for two months, but managed to see Julie in Milan on his way there.

He extended his travel to several African countries, indulging his love of travel and experiencing life in third world countries. After six months of travel Mark and Julie were reunited in the city. Two weeks later Mark proposed and after one year of knowing each other they were married. Mark states he proposed "on the strength of their letter writing."

Mark and Julie also shared strong family histories of service to others. Julie's father worked in the Public Health Service and the family moved frequently. Julie likes to point out that she went to seventeen different schools and didn't mind at all.

"Each time we moved I got to start over. I always thought, 'this time I'm going to be a perfect person.'"

Mark grew up in a religious family. His father, the hospital administrator for Grant hospital in Columbus, Ohio, died suddenly at age 69. His estate plan influenced Mark's thinking and life enormously in that 20% went to charity. Mark's charitable giving started early. During his African tour he met a missionary in Liberia who impressed him so much that he and Julie "scraped" to send regular donations to him during their early years together.

After their marriage Mark was drafted into the military and assigned to Japan, where they both witnessed the early buildup for the Vietnam War. This left a lasting impression. Caring for wounded soldiers coming back influenced Mark's pursuit of orthopedic surgery.

Both Julie and Mark enjoyed their adventures in Japan and other Asian travels. Julie's love of change made her the perfect partner for Mark. He completed his four year residency at Duke University in North Carolina where Julie worked. Eventually they settled down to suburban life in Western Massachusetts and raised four successful children (a banker, two nurse practitioners, and a teacher).

Mark's impulse to help the disadvantaged continued to grow with his successful career. "We're so blessed in our lives and we're enormously grateful for all we have. When I see things that aren't fair, I have to do something."

In 1981, influenced by her time in Japan, Julie found herself remembering the Vietnam War and injustice to the Vietnamese people. She persuaded Mark to let a family of Vietnamese boat people live in their basement for several months. They welcomed this family of six including a husband and wife, one daughter and two sons, and a grandmother. The decision raised a few eyebrows in their conservative, affluent community. Later they bought a house for the Vietnamese family, which Mark and Julie later donated to the church. The family thrived and their daughter eventually graduated from Boston College.

In 1995, Mark began volunteering as a physician in Viet Nam. Julie went with him and unsuccessfully tried to encourage the Vietnamese to adopt the concept of visiting nurses.

In 1999, Mark joined their church's outreach project with Haiti, never imagining what a life changing experience this would become. He visited Port-au-Prince, Haiti, with his pastor and other church members to dedicate the school his church generously donated. There he saw opportunities for collaboration, sending medical supplies, and lending technical expertise. He visited almost every year and formed close friendships with Haitian pastors and school administrators. He experienced many tragedies with the Haitian people: the 2010 earthquake which flattened the school and killed

20 student nurses, the kidnapping and murder of the pastor's son, and the sudden death of their pastor last year at 53.

After that devastating earthquake, the school decided to rebuild a bigger and better place to teach children, student nurses, and theology students. Mark donated funds for them to purchase land beside the destroyed school. The school and supporting organizations insisted on honoring Mark and naming the Dr. Pohlman Park after him.

In addition to the support in Haiti, both Julie and Mark supported environmental causes. They were inspired by Middlebury professor Bill McKibben, an American environmentalist who co-founded 350.org and works to make communities more sustainable.

Throughout their marriage Mark and Julie peppered their good works, medical professions, and child rearing with plenty of fun. They built a house in the Adirondacks where they live from June to October and where, for many years, they enjoyed sailing and kayaking.

Health problems make aging difficult for Julie and she keenly misses active sports. She fondly remembers her years of skiing, sailing, biking, and tennis. Mark has been more fortunate and last year was the first winter he didn't ski.

Mark and Julie have occupied a condo for 17 years. Mark retired soon after they moved in, which Julie admits was distracting for her. Eventually he moved his office to an upstairs loft and decreased the mess underfoot.

"What retirement advice would you give others?" I asked.

Mark said, "Always keep your mind open to do new things, and keep busy. Think about what you can do and what you value. I never imagined all the things I've done to promote education and the environment. Being a physician brings respect and I can use my influence to accomplish things." Julie and Mark's final words of advice for people of retirement age:

Julie: "Be willing to take risks!"

Mark: "Keep an open mind and opportunities will present themselves."

Thank you, Julie and Mark for sharing your inspirational lives and generosity to others.

Young Julie and Mark Pohlman *Mark and Julie Pohlman 50th Anniversary*

My Five Year Plan
Kathy
(Patricia)

> *"If you're going through hell, keep going."*
> *Winston Churchill*

How can we carry on when a spouse's terminal illness causes retirement plans to crash and burn? Kathy's story shows how one strong woman coped by devising a five year plan. Her life speaks to the need for flexibility and resilience as we face the unavoidable—and sometimes catastrophic—changes that are part of life, especially during our later years.

Kathy was born and raised in the South, a middle child who spent most of her life near Oxford, Mississippi. Her father worked as a civil engineer and her mother stayed at home with the children. After graduating from Ole Miss, Kathy worked her way up to a job with a congressman in Washington, D.C for two years, then returned to Oxford as a recruiter for Ole Miss.

After leaving a six-year relationship, Kathy felt wary about jumping back into the dating cycle. She recalls, My boss and his wife wanted me to meet a young attorney named Bill at a party they were having. I arrived on time, but Bill came late. I already felt awkward as the youngest person there, and when Bill finally arrived he talked with other people and mostly ignored me. I hung to the side, nursing one beer after another. We drank wine at dinner and conversation continued to flow around me. After dinner I was horrified to feel drunk at my boss's house, in front of professors I saw professionally each day. I locked myself in the upstairs bathroom and lay on the floor with a cold cloth on my head until I felt better. When I came downstairs everyone was gone except my boss, his wife, and Bill, who were sitting on the front steps. They quickly said goodnight and went inside, leaving me alone with Bill. At that point I desperately wanted to go home, but Bill regaled me with stories about his law practice.

He was a wonderful raconteur, but after 20 minutes I excused myself and drove home thinking, 'I'll never see that guy again and I just hope I don't get fired on Monday.'

The next day Bill called to apologize for not being more attentive and asked if I'd go fishing with him that afternoon. I surprised myself by saying yes. I decided to give him a second chance because the botched first date was half my fault.

"And so began an unlikely but wonderful relationship that lasted 36 years. We married about two years later and lived in Clarksdale, Mississippi where Bill was an attorney and I attended law school at Ole Miss. Later we moved to Memphis, Tennessee, where we raised our three children and I stayed home with them. When our youngest entered high school I worked at various jobs and ended as Director of Children's Ministry at Grace St. Luke Episcopal Church." The years flew by, the children grew up, and when Bill's job changed he began thinking about retirement and moving back to Oxford. At first Kathy opposed the move, though they already had a weekend house there. But someone wanted to buy their house and fate seemed to point them toward home.

She says, Bill was so happy in Oxford. He looked forward to being retired from regular work, but hoped to start a consulting business. We found a great house on a lake that met all Bill's retirement needs: an excellent golf course, a lake to fish on every day, wonderful friends not far away, the dream of traveling with me several times a year, a university with sports to love, and a business department with opportunities for meaningful volunteer work.

All was well for Bill, but I wanted a job to establish a life of my own, although I needed to stay flexible with time off for travel. Through one of Bill's high school friends I found a teaching job at the Methodist church preschool. They hired me two days later to help in the three your old room in the mornings, with summers off.

"Life was perfect, or so it seemed. But our carefree life lasted only six months."

"What happened?" I asked.

Our world changed in September, 2014 when Bill was diagnosed with idiopathic pulmonary fibrosis—a disease with a two to five year survival rate, with no chance of recovery. He lasted only seven months, dying in April, 2015.

"He enjoyed that one year of retirement—volunteering at Ole Miss, mentoring young entrepreneurs, fishing, and enjoying friends and his dogs on our deck with a martini in hand. He couldn't play golf, but could drive the cart for our son as he played. We got in two good trips, but mostly we savored the ordinary days of life with each other."

"How did you cope with his death?" I asked.

"Grief counseling helped a lot. I originally started counseling in Memphis before we left because I was grieving the losses I would experience in the move. Bill loved Oxford and had always wanted to retire there; he never completely sold me on the idea. I loved our house in Memphis and my yard was my workplace. It was beginning to have that old garden feel. I saw a grief counselor, Bob, about twice a month for four months. That positive experience helped me with the move. When Bill was diagnosed with the terminal illness, I called Bob and asked him to see Bill and me as a couple. He agreed, but we only had one session with him. Still, it was a good session and gave us a roadmap to start the journey. Bob asked Bill about his greatest fear at that time. He answered with tears running down his face that he knew the time would come when we'd have an argument, and he didn't want to waste any of our time together in a disagreement. This statement stayed with me and I don't think we exchanged a disagreeable word for the next seven months. When we felt angry or frustrated, each of us took time alone until we could address the situation."

"Did you and Bill discuss what you'd do after his death?" I asked.

Kathy shook her head. We never talked about it. I know Bill saw me as a strong, independent person and had confidence I'd find my way. Both our mothers were widowed fairly early and led successful lives afterward.

Really, I had no idea how hard it would be to go forward without Bill. I don't think there was an answer to that question, 'What will happen to me?' I believe the answer lies in the decisions I make each day to move forward.

"As a friend reminds me when I'm deep in the grief hole: 'You aren't the only person this has ever happened to. Remember that!'"

"Did you continue with counseling?"

"Yes. After our one session with Bob, who was leaving the area for a long trip, I searched for another counselor and asked Bill to do the same. We found John, who had just opened a limited practice in Oxford. First I met with John alone, and then we saw him as a couple. John and Bill were instant friends and he looked forward to the sessions each week. I felt a bit left out as their relationship deepened, but I did enjoy the sessions and Bill and I always had better conversations when we left."

"What were your conversations about?" I asked.

Mostly we didn't talk about death—we talked about living life with intention and making good decisions about the time we had together. Bill's father had died when Bill was about the same age as our own children. From that experience, Bill felt our kids would be fine because they had good lives with promising futures, and it's in the natural order for parents to die.

"After he died the children and I had one meeting with John, which felt awkward. I don't recommend taking your children to see a counselor as a group."

"Did you continue with counseling?" I asked.

Kathy said, I saw John for six months after Bill's death. During those sessions he encouraged me to take things slowly and not make any major decisions for at least a year. He also suggested I should have a daily plan so I could feel a sense of control in my life. And, I should stay connected to friends.

"John and I talked about painful feelings Bill and I couldn't discuss without someone urging us onward. Fortunately, I was a 61 year old woman in good health, with a solid financial base. I continued sessions with John and, based on what I had read about grief and discussed with him, I kept doing everything my energy level would support."

"I know it's different for everyone," I said, "but how long did your recovery take?"

"For a year after Bill's death I stayed in a fog most days—still practicing magical thinking that if I did everything just right my life would go back to the way it was. I stayed in that fog during most of my daughter's wedding plans that fall, but was able to oversee things with the help of good friends and my daughter's clear thinking."

She sighed. "The retirement life I planned with Bill was no longer available, so I came up with a five year plan to help me look to the future and feel like I had a small grip on it."

"Why five years?" I asked.

"There was no magic in the number five, but it felt like a manageable amount of time. I'd never kept the same job for five years, so I told myself I'd keep my job in Oxford for five years and then reevaluate. That decision took pressure off of me about making big changes and gave me a framework of the immediate future. I would have a home in Oxford with summers off to travel, visit children, and other things."

"And how did things go for you?"

"It's a good thing I didn't make any sudden changes. Oxford wasn't my first choice for retirement because I wanted to live near at least one of our children, but now I love the lake house—partly because Bill loved it and we lived here together."

She added, Besides that, I didn't have the mental or physical energy to make a move. Also, I needed peace and calm, a space for healing and acceptance—I needed to quit worrying about what would happen to me.

"That five years of being with three-year-old children was a perfect way for helping me stay in the moment. They don't remember yesterday and have little concept of tomorrow—it's all about the present moment. When I'd start worrying, I reminded myself 'This is your five year plan. Just be here for now.'"

"What keeps you active besides work?" I asked.

"Lots of things. I'm finishing a screened porch for the house, spending time with my children in Idaho and San Francisco, exploring the Oxford community, developing a garden plan, and doing various hobbies. I also want to devote more time to exercise and continue with my yoga practice."

"And the future?"

"At the end of five years I might move to be near the children, or I could just stay here if it feels like home. My future is still out there to be discovered."

"What advice do you have for other widows or widowers?"

Every life is unique, but I can say what worked for me. Utter confusion is what I felt after Bill died, even though I knew it was coming. That's a normal way to feel, I learned. Nothing can quite prepare a person for being alone after a death.

"I advise people to take time and be intentional about their journeys. Don't rush. On days when I feel loneliness I don't ignore it. I acknowledge the sadness, wallow in it for a brief time, and then follow with some radical self-love."

"What does self-love look like for you?" I asked.

"For me, it can be a visit to the spa for a great pedicure, a long walk in the woods with my dogs, or staying in bed reading all day without feeling guilty about it. But, this is two and a half years after Bill's death, so it's easier to distract myself."

"What about during the early period?"

Kathy shook her head, remembering. During the first year I spent a lot of time in bed staring out the window. But I kept my job, which forced me to get out of bed for at least five hours a day. Having something meaningful to do is different for each person—an exercise class, a pet, a grandchild, a volunteer activity. I found as each day went by and the world kept turning, I kept getting up one more time.

My biggest help besides my children were three good friends who called or took my calls every week; a good therapist I could see as needed; reading everything I could find on grief—blogs, books, articles, listening to podcasts—and crying and crying and crying.

"Even two years out, on some days I see no reason to keep going. My latest coping method comes from an article I read about the law of motion: An object at rest tends to stay at rest, and an object in motion tends to stay in motion. When you feel unable to function, just tell yourself you only have to make one movement and that movement will help the next movement, etc. This works amazingly well for me right now."

Kathy has found coping mechanisms that work for her, yet she realizes this journey can take years. She recently said, "My grief is less raw and painful now; it's more like chronic pain. You learn ways to cope and keep a smile on your face as you proceed forward."

Godspeed on your journey forward, Kathy.

NOTES

Grief Counseling

The world changes when we lose a spouse, and it's normal to feel numb, shocked, and afraid. Some people feel guilt for being the one still alive, or anger at the spouse for leaving. There are no rules for how we should feel. There is no right or wrong way to mourn. During this difficult time grief counseling and a support group can help you process feelings, make plans for the future, and just get through each day. The National Institute on Aging offers excellent information about mourning the death of a spouse: https://www.nia.nih.gov/health/mourning-death-spouse

Small Steps and the Law of Inertia

The method Kathy speaks of is recommended by clinical psychologist Robert Maurer in his book, *One Small Step Can Change Your Life*. In this book he explores the Japanese concept of *kaizen*, which is about small steps. Kaizen is a method of asking ourselves, "What is the simplest thing I can do to begin moving?" Easily achievable goals that are small do not trigger the amygdala to go into alert mode, and without this fear we are able to adapt and change one small step at a time.

Other Resources

The On Being Project Blog, https://onbeing.org. Kathy listens to this weekly.

Mary Catherine Bateson, *Composing a Further Life - The Age of Active Wisdom*, Vintage Publishing, 2011.

Joan Didion, *The Year of Magical Thinking*. Vintage Publishing, 2007.

Joan Didion , *Blue Nights*. Vintage Publishing, 2012.

Robert Maurer, *One Small Step Can Change Your Life: The Kaizen Way*. New York: Workman, 2004.

Who Am I Now?

Adrienne Plotkin

(Helene)

> *"All successful people, men and women, are big dreamers.*
> *They imagine what their future could be, ideal in every*
> *respect, and then they work every day toward their distant*
> *vision, that goal or purpose."*
> Brian Tracy from Personal Success

While her friends and neighbors lived suburban lives, managing their homes, tending their children, and working locally, Adrienne—a sophisticated dark haired beauty—commuted to Boston and held a high powered administrative position with the Massachusetts Department of Mental Health.

Adrienne's husband Bob is a beloved retired pediatrician with an office in Longmeadow, not far from their home. He's known for patience, kindness, gorgeous brown eyes and an engaging smile. Adrienne took comfort knowing he was nearby as she (with his blessing and pride) pursued her career goals. They had six children. Few people know their third child died tragically at three months of age of a SIDS death.

All these children came to a couple who doubted they'd be able to have children. Adrienne recalls she loved being pregnant.

"Why was that?" I asked.

"Miscarrying my first pregnancy taught me to value each one, which gave me an incredible sense of well-being. Children were important to me and Bob: he was an only child and I had only one brother."

Adrienne and Leonard (Bobby) met while he was in medical school and she worked in a research laboratory for Tufts University.

Bob earned extra money employed in the same laboratory and they bonded over a sea of urine specimens arranged according to their various hues. "Not exactly a romantic scene," Adrienne says.

After their marriage in 1953 when he was 29 and she 21, the couple moved to Longmeadow, Massachusetts and, as her children started coming along, Adrienne dove head long into volunteer activities: Springfield museums, Springfield Symphony, Wesson Maternity Hospital, and a Boy Scout leader. She was also the first president of the community mental health center.

Over the years she held many positions that monitored mental health, mental retardation, drug abuse, and children's community services throughout Massachusetts. Her quality assurance responsibilities and administrative duties gradually increased and put her in contact with citizen boards, constituency groups, legislators, and media sources. At one point she co-anchored a public television show in Boston where she interviewed prominent people and provided information about advocacy and patient's rights.

Community outreach was Adrienne's expertise. When the state of Massachusetts struggled with changes brought on by deinstitutionalizing the mentally ill, she helped develop a program for monitoring 17 state in-patient and out-patient facilities. She worked closely with the Mass. Alliance of the Mentally Ill.

As Adrienne gets lost in the details of her lengthy and impressive professional life, she dwells on the satisfaction of mentoring interns who went on to accomplish great things. One became a staff member in the Obama White House. Another, an African American woman she encouraged to pursue further education, attended law school at the same time she was director of human rights for the state.

"Did Bob always support your career?" I asked.

"Absolutely! He said a happy, productive wife makes for a happy life. One of the best parts of my job was having an apartment across the street from the Statehouse in Boston. Bob and I sometimes spent weekends together there to enjoy Boston and relive memories of his medical school and our early years together."

Adrienne and Bob's five children remain active in their lives—supportive, helpful in emergencies, and very close. Adrienne and Bob also have ten grandchildren. Their oldest son is a psychiatrist and the youngest is an attorney in Boston. One of their daughters, a successful realtor in Arizona, introduced them to the warm winters of that state. They eventually bought a second home one mile from their daughter.

After working for the state for 34 years, Adrienne retired in 2010. Bob had already retired in 2003 after practicing medicine for 54 years. As she deals with the aches and pains of getting older, Bob offers gentle support. Anxiety comes over Adrienne's beautiful face when she thinks of their aging: "I don't like thinking about what's to come. I miss being young and active."

Loss of identify is a problem for her since retirement. She says, "First I was a wife, mother, volunteer, and ultimately Boston Area Human Rights Coordinator of the Department of Mental Health. I miss the decision making power I had, the people I worked with, and the structure. I didn't feel productive after I retired, and that affected my self-worth. I lost many relationships."

"I never thought about retirement beforehand," she adds.

However, Adrienne identified when she read the story of my own retirement journey in *The Other Couch: Discovering Women's Wisdom in Therapy*. She told me, "Your chapter made me think about the need for planning ahead and identifying new challenges, projects I could be passionate about."

Adrienne admits she gets caught up with recrimination and regrets I should have focused more on opportunities to develop my talents after retirement.

"PLAN AHEAD!" is Adrienne's advice for future retirees. "Think about what you can do to stay active, feel useful, and maintain your identity—if that's what you want."

My interview with Adrienne gave us a chance to explore a new friendship and we discovered our careers overlapped for many years. I evaluated and treated some of the patients in Western Massachusetts who were impacted by her work to protect them. We experienced the impact of de-institutionalization from opposite poles. We worked with some of the same professionals, yet never knew each other. And, her kindhearted Bobby was our children's pediatrician.

Our conversation spurred Adrienne to think about how she can use her experience with retirement to help others. Adrienne will never cease being a planner, a person looking for the big picture, a coordinator, and an inspiration to others. Yet, she failed to plan her own future—perhaps because focusing on herself doesn't come easily. Since her mother lived to be 95, we hope Adrienne has plenty of time to figure things out.

Postscript: Adrienne and I had several conversations following the initial interview. She tells me, "After our talks, I spent several sleepless nights thinking about my lack of passion.

"Then, my life's passion jumped into my head while I lay awake at night, thinking instead of sleeping. What was the most exciting, satisfying, and rewarding time of my adult and professional life? It came from working in human rights with adult patients.

"I now realize this is the time for me to channel that passion. Thank you, Helene, for turning my life in a productive direction."

Shortly after gaining an improved sense of direction, Adrienne became very ill and had to put her plans for activist work on hold. We wish her improved health and years of happy, productive living.

Adrienne Plotkin in retirement. Sadly, the world lost Adrienne on September 27, 2018.

Occupational Wellness

Loonacy in Retirement

John and Kittie Wilson
(Patricia)

> *"Only in quiet waters do things mirror themselves undistorted. Only in a quiet mind is adequate perception of the world." Hans Margolius*

> *"Sometimes, the prettiest smiles hide the deepest secrets. The prettiest eyes have cried the most tears. And the kindest hearts have felt the most pain." anonymous*

I love watching for loons during the summer on Lake Sunapee in New Hampshire. On many afternoons our family of eight loads into the boat, with snacks and drinks, to search for the loons in special coves we discovered. It's such a treat to spot one, then two loons, sometimes with baby chicks riding on their parents' backs. Even more special is watching our three grandchildren when we find a loon. They learned to stay quiet, and when we give the okay they mimic the loon call. Even Lilly at just under two years of age knows how to make the loon wail, "oo-oo-oo." The pure, mournful tones break to a higher pitch and then down again.

So when I learned Kittie Wilson would be giving a presentation about her twelve year observances of loons on Pleasant Lake, I had to attend. Kittie opened her talk by saying she and her husband John were having a great deal of fun being absolutely loony in retirement.

"Aha," I told myself. "Here's a couple who found a special hobby/ avocation in their retirement. I need to put them in the book."

When I entered their beautiful home on the lake, a loon immediately appeared at the window. Next I saw hummingbirds, goldfinches, and a darting chipmunk. Their home felt like an Eden of flora and fauna.

John is 75 and Kittie 68, but they seem younger, with ready smiles and healthy physiques. Each of them has blue eyes and white hair. John has sailed most of his life and they both still enjoy sailing and downhill skiing.

Kittie was an elementary school teacher in New London, NH, for 31 years, while John was the dentist in town for 32 years. For fifteen years Kittie served as an enrichment teacher, offering a course called Mindstretch that taught the students creativity, critical thinking and problem solving. She loved this work and received the Christa McAuliffe Award for Excellence in Teaching.

After 28 years of marriage—a second marriage for each of them—Kittie and John still have deep love and respect for each other. They seem a perfect match, like the pair of loons they've observed for the past twelve years; peaceful and calm, with purpose.

They began putting away money for retirement years earlier, but didn't have immediate plans to stop working until Kittie's school district started an early retirement provision at age 55. As that year approached for Kittie, John also began thinking of retirement. At 55 and 61 they left their careers to begin a new phase of life, with John having plans to fix up an old Model A truck that had been sitting in his garage for 30 years, and Kittie hoping to expand her mindstretch enrichment work to a wider audience.

They each worried about not having the structure of work or the identities of teacher and dentist.

"But to my surprise," John says, "I retired from dentistry and never looked back."

On the other hand, Kittie felt more angst about saying goodbye to teaching. She hoped that developing her enrichment program would help her feel useful. But as the months rolled by, Kittie realized she needed to put academic work behind her. She no longer felt the passion to continue.

She said, "I asked myself what would be my new identity. Prophetically, a pair of loons began nesting on Pleasant Lake. I felt their hypnotic loon song calling me, and I answered."

Now Kittie gets up early each morning when the loons are nesting and drives to a viewing blind she created to observe and photograph them. After the loons leave the nest, Kittie is on the water by 4:30 AM in her little Zodiac boat with a silent electric motor, photographing them.

"It didn't take long for us to become loon activists," Kittie says. "We joined the Loon Preservation Committee (LPC) in Moultonborough, NH. www.loon.org. We quickly learned that lead poisoning from ingesting lead sinkers and lead-headed jigs is the leading cause of death for adult common loons in New Hampshire. We've worked hard to pass NH Senate Bill 89 in 2013 to outlaw the use and sale of lead sinkers and jigs. The law went into effect in 2016."

"That must've been a challenge," I said.

Kittie and John nod. "Getting the bill passed was an arduous task, but we were determined and passionate, along with many others."

"What other loonacy are you involved in?" I asked.

John says, "As a volunteer for LPC, I build floating nests for breeding of the loons, which leads to the hatching of baby chicks every year on Pleasant Lake."

Kittie added, "I photograph the loons every year and publish a yearly loon calendar and several documentary photo books. All the profits from sales go to LPC. I also publish a weekly nature journal called 'All Things Pleasant on the Lake,' which is read by hundreds of nature lovers."

Kittie's stunning photographs and upcoming events are available to view at www.kittiewilson.com. She and John have received many awards for their conservation/preservation work.

John, who planned to restore the old Model A truck, took a welding course to prepare for the task. He enjoyed the course but never seemed to get around to repairing the truck. It sat in the garage, almost snickering at him, "So when are you going to work on me?"

He says, "Seeing the truck waiting for me every day became stressful. One day at the local coffee shop a regular asked if I still had the truck and wanted to sell it.

"I thought, *Heck, I don't really want to fix it. Why not sell it?* I felt immediate relief with that decision."

Right away an opportunity arose to join the New London Budget Committee, where he served for twelve years, five of them as chairman. John continues volunteering in town government— something he never thought of doing, but he likes being active and feeling needed, including the "good stress" of life.

"I think a certain amount of stress is healthy in retirement and keeps you alive. Facing challenges keeps you going," John says.

"What's the biggest lesson you learned from retirement?" I ask.

"Stay FLEXIBLE," they answered in unison.

Kittie adds, Don't lock yourself into following a specific plan that sounded right before retirement. You may think you'll do this or that, only to find something else comes along that piques your interest and becomes a passion—like our loons.

"I felt frightened at first without the structure of being a teacher, so I tried to be more laidback and just let the days evolve. But that wasn't my personality. I truly need structure, even as a retired person."

Now John and Kittie write a daily list of activities on a sticky note each night. The tasks might include gardening, feeding the birds and for Kittie, a boat ride out to find her loons and work on her photography. John is passionate about playing tennis twice a week, so every other appointment has to work around that commitment. They also travel and enjoy socializing with family and friends.

They say, "We feel retirement shouldn't be static. Retirement is always changing. Doors close, windows open. We work hard to be flexible, creative, and willing to pursue new paths. So, for us, retirement is all about change."

Another part of their retirement life has been adjusting to the death of John's daughter, who died in a tragic car accident when she was 23 years of age and John was 57. He credits Kittie and her strength for getting him through those first terrible years. Kittie credits John for being her support as she grieved her step-daughter. Together they decided to celebrate Jody's life, rather than stay in a constant state of mourning. They've done this by memorializing Jody in some way every year on her birthday. Their remaining son is single and lives in New York City.

John and Kittie's lives are filled with love, excitement, and adventures. "Because our 'circle of influence' is constantly growing, it creates interesting surprises that lead to new relationships, and sometimes new problems to solve. Of course, we can't foresee health issues or tragic events like the loss of loved ones."

They say, Retirement brings many opportunities, but be careful to manage your time so you don't overcommit. We find that saying no can be a challenge because we're involved with projects we feel need to be done.

"Getting older is the part we like the least. We have so many things we want to do – and so little time!"

But continuing to "do" is what Kittie and John are all about, as civic minded committee members, environmentalists, photographers, authors, guest speakers, and loon conservationists. And in "doing" they find their purpose and sense of wellbeing. As Kittie writes in her weekly nature journal:

Morning on the lake is all about quiet waters. Geese rise through wispy fog. Loons move silently to morning feeding grounds. Their minds are quiet, focused on the day and the task at hand. Perception of their world is keen and sharp and accurate. As the loons groom, their bands become visible and remind us of the loons' tolerance and goodwill as we strive to learn more about their lives.

Gardens are also wonderful places to seek to acquire a quiet mind. The floral bouquet is so warm in mid-August . . . leaving us feeling sunny and good. And while we are there, among the flowers, so are the hummingbirds! We see lots of babies now, finding their way, sipping the fresh nectar. We will enjoy searching for quiet waters in order to develop quiet minds. Nature will show us the way.

Postscript: I received a heartbreaking email from John Wilson on May 4, 2018: "It is with extraordinary sadness that I must tell you that Kittie Wilson, our Precious Loon Lady, who had an incredible zest for life, passed away on May 3." The obituary read that Kittie died with her loving husband by her side after putting up a vigorous fight against aggressive cancer.

Kittie's last blog report was on April 20, 2018, and in it she quoted F. Scott Fitzgerald: "It was only a sunny smile, and little it cost in the giving, but like morning light it scattered the night and made the day worth living."

Dear Kittie, your radiant smile and generous kindness will be missed and long remembered by all who knew you!

Kittie and John Wilson

Kittie Wilson

John Wilson

The Judge's Decision
Justice John M. Greaney
(Patricia)

"We are what we repeatedly do. Excellence, then is not an act, but a habit." –Aristotle

"I grew up poor," were the first words Justice John M. Greaney spoke when I asked if we could tell his story in this book. He reflected on his father, an Irish immigrant who left Ireland in 1923 during the Irish Civil War between the Irish Republican Army and the Free State forces. His father Patrick was a laborer who worked tough jobs to support the family.

When he first arrived in this country my father worked in 100 degree heat, doing back breaking labor, in a cast iron boiler manufacturing plant. We lived above my maternal grandmother's house in a small three room flat. We didn't own a refrigerator, a television, or a car.

"I was an only child who had the value of work instilled in me at an early age. I started formally working at age twelve, picking tobacco in fields in Connecticut. I did this every summer until I was sixteen and picked up other jobs along the way. That work ethic still motivates me to work at age seventy-nine; I want to be productive, engaged, and helpful. I enjoy what I do and making the lives of others better."

When John was in eighth grade at the local Catholic school he received invaluable advice. He hoped to attend college, but knew his family could never afford the expense. One day the Sister of St. Joseph who taught his classes told him that, every four years, the top boy academically in his Catholic high school graduating class received a scholarship to the College of the Holy Cross.

At age twelve, John recognized a golden opportunity to attend college—if he worked extremely hard in school. He did graduate as the top male student in his class and was awarded the College of the Holy Cross scholarship. The scholarship didn't cover everything, so he worked at the post office over Christmas break, and held two jobs in the summer, one during the day and one at night. He also took out loans to meet his expenses.

He studied Classics at Holy Cross (Latin and Greek in the original texts), and graduated summa cum laude. With a Classics degree Justice Greaney said, "you would either become a priest (which he didn't want to do), teach classics, or go to law school." The law interested him because of the potential for public service, but with his college debt still looming, how could he ever afford law school? Finances were always in the forefront of his modest upbringing.

He says, "It was clear to me early on that I had to work hard; I couldn't take time off. That has been a guiding principle throughout my life."

Hoping for miracles, John applied to several law schools and received acceptance letters from each of them—Harvard, Yale, Boston College, and New York University. Harvard gave him no financial aid; Yale offered a partial scholarship; and both Boston College and NYU awarded him full scholarships.

"I already had a sufficient amount of pure Catholic education, so I chose NYU. I felt more than ready for a secular school. I was fortunate to be selected as a Root-Tilden-Kern scholar, which offers a full scholarship for the three years of law school." The scholarship students were selected for their academic achievement, commitment to public service, and potential for leadership.

John defines his life by these three criteria. By the time he earned a law degree, what he learned from the nuns at his parish school, and later the Jesuits at Holy Cross, had become a strong calling. Their advice (more a philosophy of life) was this: *Each of us has a relatively short time on earth. We should therefore use our abilities to better the lives of others according to our individual talents.*

After passing the bar exam John had a military obligation to fulfill (this was still the time of the draft). While many young men sought medical deferments, protested the Viet Nam War, or headed for Canada, John met his obligation.

"It wasn't right to let other people serve and risk their lives while I evaded my patriotic duty," John explains. He enlisted in the 104th Tactical Fighter Group of the Air National Guard in Westfield, Massachusetts. He was assigned to the Judge Advocate Office at the Air Base, knowing he might be called up to active duty. (The 104th had been activated in almost every war the United States had fought). During this time he met his wife, a math teacher, and they married in 1967. They've been married for fifty-one years.

While in the National Guard, John started law practice in Springfield, Massachusetts with a medium size law firm founded by a former Governor of Massachusetts. He started as a general practitioner, handling all types of legal matters (both civil and criminal).

John knew he wanted to become a judge, but that required a minimum of ten years' law practice before seeking appointment to a judgeship. In 1974, he was selected as the first judge of the Hampden County Housing Court in Springfield, Massachusetts.

He says, "This was a huge assignment that required working days, nights, and many weekends. As only the second Housing Court in Massachusetts, the Hampden County court had to be designed and built from scratch."

John did so, and in the process fashioned many new and innovative changes to court procedure and practice—among them were court forms in plain English, forms in Spanish, and a Citizens Advisory Council to offer suggestions that would benefit the court and its users.

In 1976, the governor appointed Justice Greaney to the Superior Court, the general trial court of the Commonwealth, and in 1979, to the Appeals Court. In 1985, he was named Chief Justice of the Appeals Court. His highest honor occurred in 1990 with an appointment to the Supreme Judicial Court of Massachusetts—a position he held until mandatory retirement at age seventy in 2008.

Justice Greaney didn't feel ready for retirement at age 70. His health remained good and he still had much to offer the world. While looking for other opportunities he found a position directing the Macaronis Institute for Trial and Appellate Advocacy at Suffolk University Law School. When the institute closed in 2015, John still didn't want to retire. A local Springfield law firm asked him to join as Senior Counsel. He began this assignment on a part time basis that continues to this day. He says, "I enjoy mentoring young lawyers in the firm and working on special projects."

This philosophy and John's work ethic make him a "continuer," according to Dr. Nancy Schlossberg's model of different retirement paths. In her book, *Too Young to Be Old: Love, Learn, Work, and Play As You Age*, Dr. Schlossberg says, "*Continuers* modify their activities while continuing along a similar path. . . continuers maintain their former identity, but in a modified way. . .Continuers stay connected to their former work and their former identities while developing on new fronts." (Page 97).

"What advice do you have for other retirees who want to feel useful?" I asked.

"If you feel comfortable and competent to continue working and still have skills you can use—either paid or as a volunteer— then by all means keep going. I serve on several volunteer boards with charitable foundations, but I still feel the need to work in law."

"How would you summarize your philosophy about working so long?" I asked.

He answered with the lyrics of "Man in Black" by Johnny Cash, his favorite country singer:

"I wear black for the poor and the beaten down,

For those who live on the hungry side of town.

For those who have long since done their time,

But who are still paying for their crime."

He continues, "I wore black as a judge and, in some small way, I wanted to help people who suffered, and were still suffering from burdens inflicted by society."

For fortunate people like John Greaney, a career is more than a job; it's a calling of the heart and spirit. Being asked to quit just when we've reached the peak of experience and wisdom doesn't feel right. While many of us enjoy the freedom that comes with retirement, other retirees find meaningful work fills them with purpose, helps them stay young at heart, and allows them to give back to the community.

John's life isn't all work. He continues exercising and taking walks. Socially, he goes out with friends, attends social events, speaks to groups, and serves on charitable boards and committees. The Justice enjoys reading, especially historical books about Irish history, in particular the Irish Uprising of 1916.

This humble yet accomplished man has changed the course of many lives with his fair judgment and humanitarian wisdom. He is a role model for those who want to continue working into their seventies, and perhaps their eighties.

Justice Greaney is the kind of senior citizen you'd love to meet over a cup of coffee and hear reflections about the past, plus his wise opinions about the present and future. I thank him for allowing me to share his story.

NOTES

Nancy K. Schlossberg, Ed.D., *Too Young To Be Old: Love, Learn, Work, and Play As You Age*. American Psychological Association, Washington, D.C., 2017.

Another Job Before I Volunteer

Bill Stromquist

(Patricia)

"As you grow older, you will discover that you have two hands — one for helping yourself, the other for helping others." Audrey Hepburn

"Volunteers are the only human beings on the face of the earth who reflect this nation's compassion, unselfish caring, patience, and just plain loving one another." Erma Bombeck

I met Bill Stromquist at my book signing event at the Pensacola Southwest Branch Library. He came to the event because he saw I was a Purdue graduate, where he attended school for several years. We enjoyed reminiscing about Purdue and Lafayette, Indiana, and then he asked to buy ten books. That's a big purchase! When I asked why so many books, Bill said he knew women who needed to read the stories in *The Other Couch*.

A year later I gave a public talk on domestic violence and introduced my new book, *Liars, Cheats and Creeps*. Again, Bill attended the event and bought ten books for "friends who will benefit from the stories." I realized this man was a kind, generous soul who not only helped me market my books but was like Robin Hood, caring for others.

When he told me about his life, I knew his story needed to be in this book, because Bill Stromquist is a perfect example of occupational wellness. He began working at age 16, then found a career he loved and stuck with it for thirty years. At retirement he took another job for ten years before retiring at 62 to do volunteer work.

Bill grew up in Amesbury, Massachusetts, living with his father and paternal grandparents until he was eleven years of age. He moved in with his grandparents while his father served in World War II and his mother pursued a career as a big band singer in New York City. He speaks of happy days in Amesbury with his father and uncles, all WW II veterans.

When Bill was eleven his father remarried a fifth grade schoolteacher, the total opposite of his mother except for one thing: She too had no interest in being Bill's mother. As Bill puts it, "She was too mean to have children."

She left his grandparents to raise Bill and resented any attention he got from his father. Bill says, "She called me the "Bookless Wonder" because I didn't bring home books to study, yet I still made good grades. I buried myself in sports during high school."

He played football, basketball, and was named an All New England catcher in baseball. Bill looks back on this part of his life without resentment, saying, "I'm glad my father was happy in the marriage, even if I didn't get to have a mother."

After high school, Bill wanted to find his real mother, who'd been missing from his life for so many years. She lived in Miami, so he boarded an airplane for the first time. Inauspiciously, the plane made a crash landing, blowing out the tires and ending up in the grass off the runway farthest from the terminal. "It was dramatic," he says, "especially because the actor Vic Damone was also on the plane."

Once he reached the waiting room, Bill immediately recognized his mother. He spent the summer there and kept in contact with her for 15 more years, but the relationship ended when her alcoholism and self-centered attitude created too much drama in his life.

After high school, Bill worked at various jobs instead of going to college, "because I didn't want to take my stepmother's money for school." Instead, he became independent at a young age. He always remembered his dad and uncles saying, "If we'd stayed in the military, we'd be retired by now." That message stuck in his head, so when his draft number was about to come up at age 21, he enlisted in the Navy. He knew then he was going to retire— in twenty years! He would be a Navy man and train in aviation electronics. Before his slot was open for training in Memphis, he was assigned to Pensacola Naval Air Station. For six months he worked at grunt jobs, but he says "I loved the Pensacola area, and thought I might retire there."

Throughout his Navy career, Bill played on various bowling teams and fast pitch softball teams. The officers kept him from transferring when they saw his skill as a batter and pitcher, which landed him in Corpus Christi, Texas, for three years. There he met his first wife, who was also in the Navy.

Bill re-enlisted at age 25 and worked toward a degree from Purdue University through the Navy Enlisted Scientific Education Program (NESEP). He did well academically, but his wife depleted their bank account. After a couple of years at Purdue he was forced to quit school due to indebtedness; shortly thereafter they divorced after three years of marriage.

At 28 years of age he moved to Jacksonville, Florida, and began a flight deck career on naval carriers. He remembers the chief of the Lexington naval carrier asking him how he felt on the deck. "Are you scared?" asked the old chief.

To which, Bill replied, "Yeah, I am."

The Chief said, "Good. If you're ever up here and not scared, then get off the flight deck. Stay alert and keep your head on a swivel. If you're up here and complacent you can be a dead man."

Bill always remembered those words.

During his 20 year military career Bill had three more marriages. He was always kind to the women, but found himself jilted in one way or another. One woman went back to her ex-husband, another cheated on him, and the third wouldn't make the move to Pensacola. During one marriage, Bill adopted his wife's four children, whom he continued to support for seven years after the divorce. He stays in touch with some of those children.

His one regret is never having had a marriage that lasted. "I've been all around the world in the Navy, but I didn't have anyone to travel with me." He says, "I am either really stupid or a hopeless romantic. I'll go with a hopeless romantic." When asked would he marry again, he responds, "Why wouldn't I marry again?"

I guess he is a hopeless romantic, and I wish him well in that department.

When Bill retired from the Navy at 41 years of age, he started working with government contracts, earning twice what he made in the Navy. He would run the aviation division as a civilian. In Pensacola he ran the maintenance division for aircraft. He did this contract work for seven years after retirement.

Bill had reached his ultimate goal from 25 years earlier: Retirement from the Navy with full benefits. While in Pensacola he joined community activities, including the zoo, the chamber of commerce, and environmental projects.

When the position came up for Executive Director of the Chamber of Commerce, a friend suggested Bill was a natural for the job. At 52 years of age Bill took on a new challenge. He'd been working since age 16 and saw no reason to stop now. And a fantastic job he did at the Chamber.

"It was fun. I didn't do it for the $6.00 an hour pay check, which went up to $7.00 after three months. I did it because I could help people start businesses, promote the Perdido Key area, and be involved with environmental concerns. I thought the job would be fun—and it was."

For ten years he remained Executive Director and his final year included helping with the clean-up from Hurricane Ivan. He led the Emergency Operation Center for Escambia County.

"I was getting a chamber salary to train and manage the contractors. It took up to four months getting water and electricity back to the area. This was a tough job, at times working with caustic people. I stayed for a year after the hurricane to make sure everything got back to normal."

How lucky Perdido Key was to benefit from Bill's service and dedication! At 62 he retired again. Shortly thereafter, the Chamber of Commerce asked him to join the board as treasurer.

Now 74 years old, Bill has spent the last 12 years in volunteer service. He says, "I've always loved volunteering my time. In high school I taught special needs teenagers how to bowl; I was in Boy Scouts; and I was president of the Catholic Youth Organization, even though I'm not Catholic."

Bill now serves as chairman of the Perdido Key Area Chamber of Commerce, president of the Friends of Southwest Branch Library, the longest serving board member of the Gulf Shores Zoo board, and vice chairman of the Escambia County Board of Adjustments.

"How would you define your retirement?" I asked him.

"My definition of retirement is doing things I want to do, while helping people at the same time. For example, I love animals so I follow that passion by serving on the zoo board. While I've been on that board we were featured on *Animal Planet* as The Little Zoo that Could. I'm proud of that accomplishment."

"What advice do you have for future retirees?" I asked.

First, be as close to debt free as possible before you retire. If your entire pension goes to paying outstanding bills, then you won't be able to fully enjoy retirement.

"Second, retire to a place you enjoy that makes sense for you. For me, I didn't want to shovel snow and I wanted to be near a military base where I have access to a hospital, an exchange, and a pharmacy."

The can-do attitude Bill had to develop during his youth serves him well in retirement. He faces health issues, but rolls with the problems and carries on. He lost one leg below the knee to complications of diabetes, yet in the four years I've known him, I never realized he wore a prosthesis.

"I got lucky," he told me. "The surgeon who removed my leg was a noted battlefield surgeon and I never had a problem. They told me I'd walk with crutches for three or four months and wouldn't be able to use a prosthesis for at least a year. Well, I was off crutches in two weeks and back on "my feet" within a month. The leg isn't going to grow back, so what are your options? You can sit in a corner and cry, or move on. I decided to move on."

Bill is a man of great kindness and generosity who, without much nurturing love from his own family, grew into a person who deeply cares for others and his community. He demonstrates a retirement of giving back and doing for others, while still enjoying the fruits of retirement years.

Thank you Bill, for your service to others and the Perdido Key area!

Bill Stromquist at Zoo Groundbreaking

NOTES

For many senior citizens like Bill, retirement has become an active phase of life where we devote time and energy to causes and pastimes that previously took a backseat in our lives. There's no shortage of volunteer opportunities available for those who wish to donate their time and efforts during retirement. Most organizations are delighted to receive the life experience, positive energy, and professional knowledge of retirees.

In his book, *Live Long, Die Short: A Guide to Authentic Health and Successful Aging*, Roger Landry, M.D. asserts that "Our Masterpiece Living data shows that volunteerism improves memory and the ability to provide help and support to peers. We are very pleased to see volunteerism rates consistently twice as high in our successful aging communities compared to national norms." (page 164).

Roger Landry, M.D., *Live Long, Die Short: A Guide to Authentic Health and Successful Aging*, Greenleaf Book Group Press, Austin, Texas, 2014.

I'm Just Getting Good at What I Do: The Decision Not to Retire

Patricia McWade

(Patricia)

> *"Your work is going to fill a large part of your life, and the only way to be truly satisfied is to do what you believe is great work. And the only way to do great work is to love what you do. If you haven't found it yet, keep looking. Don't settle. As with all matters of the heart, you'll know when you find it."* — Steve Jobs

I have known Patricia McWade for over 20 years as the Dean of the Office of Student Financial Services at my alma mater, Georgetown University. I've always been impressed by her depth of knowledge and generosity of spirit to all students, especially those in the Georgetown Scholarship Program.

When she heard about this book, Patricia asked if I'd spoken with anyone who has no plans to retire.

"I hadn't thought of that," I told her. "Are you one of those people?"

"Absolutely!" she responded. "I'm at the top of my game now. I know more about financial aid than ever, and I help so many students. I'm not married, no children or grandchildren, and I love what I do. Why would I retire?"

"You should definitely be in the book," I told her. "I'm sure you aren't the only person who feels this way." So here is Pat's fascinating story of courage, persistence, tenacity and the wisdom to answer a true calling.

Pat was born into a lower income family in working class Malden, Massachusetts. Her parents met during the Second World

War. Her tall, handsome father was injured before deployment and received a medical discharge from the Marines. He missed going to Iwo Jima and every member of his platoon was killed there.

Pat says, "I think this affected the rest of his life and he turned to drink. He died at age 46, leaving my mother with two children at home to raise."

Pat goes on to say, "School was one of the best things about my childhood—Immaculate Conception Elementary School and Girls Catholic High School in Malden. The School Sisters of Notre Dame nuns encouraged me so much. I stayed at the top of my class and became class president for several years."

"What about college?" I asked.

She sighed. My father didn't encourage me and we had no money. He said it was a waste of time; that I should just be a damn secretary. But I was determined. I found Salem State College where I could attend for $100 a semester.

"The classes weren't challenging enough, so as sophomores a friend and I applied to Northeastern University and were accepted. I worked part time as a bank teller and also in the financial aid office to pay my tuition."

"So your financial aid experience goes way back," I commented.

"Yes, my career in financial aid started in 1967 and has continued ever since, although it wasn't my initial choice. I majored in English literature and planned to teach. But one semester of student teaching showed me I wasn't a good fit for that career. I wasn't sure what I'd do next, but I didn't worry. I always knew myself and I felt I could find my way."

Just before graduation Pat asked her supervisor at the bank if she could enroll in the bank management training program. This was 1970. They told Pat, "We don't have women in the management program, but you're welcome to stay on as a teller."

"I was angry," Pat recalls. "But I didn't give up on the idea of leadership. I turned to the Northeastern Financial Aid office where I worked during college. I started a fulltime job there right after graduation, as an administrative assistant. Within six months they promoted me to Assistant Director."

Pat says, "My goal was to help others make sense of the black box of this business we call student financial services. I knew I could write, handle finances, communicate well, and help students navigate the maze of financial aid.

"In those days we had paper files up to the ceiling with 40,000 Northeastern students and 90 percent of them received financial aid. I loved it!"

When an Associate Director position became available, she applied. During the job interview, her boss asked, "Do you know what I'm looking for?"

Pat gave a thorough, rational response about the needs of the position and how she could fulfill those requirements, but the boss dismissively replied, "I'm looking for a "yes man."

"I was stunned," Pat recalls. "But, I stayed in my position as Assistant Director because I loved the job and was learning so much."

In 1972 the Equal Pay Act passed and Pat discovered her salary was half of what men earned in the same position. When she asked her boss about this inequity, he dismissed her complaint. She stood up and said, "I'll need to take this to your boss."

Within a week, Pat spoke to the Vice President of Finances at the university and her salary doubled. Such is the tenacity and spirit of Patricia McWade, a true pioneer for women in the work force.

After seven years at Northeastern, Pat's colleagues advised her to apply for a job at the Harvard graduate school. With a blue collar background, her first response was, "I don't want to work with those snobs." But, she applied anyway and was pleasantly surprised by the men who interviewed her. "They were regular people and very nice and supportive of me."

She got the job and says, "At first I felt out of my comfort zone. They hired me to direct the Graduate Financial Aid program at Harvard, with 50 Masters and Ph.D. programs; and I was just 30 years old. But I took on the challenge and stayed at Harvard from 1979 to 1990 as the Associate Dean of Graduate Admissions and Financial Aid.

"My motto has always been, 'What do I need to learn next?' I always put myself out there and keep on going."

During a sabbatical year in 1989, Pat published a book entitled *Financing Graduate School: How to Get Money You Need for Your Graduate School Education.* While in Washington DC, Pat learned about a job at Georgetown University.

She says, Again, I wasn't sure this would be a good fit, because I had stereotypes about Catholic Universities, but I interviewed anyway. So much of my success has been due to colleagues and friends who encouraged me to take the next step.

I interviewed with a ten person search committee in a blasé manner, not sure I even wanted the job of Financial Aid Director for Georgetown University. After the day-long interview the Associate Provost asked to speak with me privately. She had many questions about my education with the School Sisters of Notre Dame, and I discovered she was a former School Sister of Notre Dame. She liked my spunk and values.

They offered me the job within a week—and that was a big decision for me. I'd be leaving the Boston area for the first time in my life, including my support network. Yet I knew it was time to take on the next challenge.

"However, I wanted to make sure my title was not Director of Financial Aid, but rather Dean of the Office of Student Financial Services. I had risen to Associate Dean level at Harvard. They agreed on the title of Dean and I began my career at Georgetown in 1991. I'm still there, 27 years later."

Pat made tremendous strides for the Financial Aid Office at Georgetown University. She improved customer service and again explained in an understandable way the maze of college financial aid. She has worked with thousands of students, many of whom continue to stay in contact with Pat. She has been instrumental in assisting in developing the Georgetown Scholarship Program, with scholarships for many first generation college students.

"Although, I never married and had my own children, I feel like many of the financial aid recipients at Georgetown are my family. It is a joy to come to work every day and I feel I do something of great value helping students find ways to support their college education. I am a first generation college student, who scraped my way through college, so I can well relate to their situation in life. I think they know that."

When asked about her thoughts of retiring Pat says it wouldn't be a productive use of her time and expertise to step out now.

"At this point in time I have the most to offer. With fifty years in the business I've developed a reputation and network that can aid students. I need to invest daily in staying current on all topics in financial services; I still love it and feel on top of my game. I don't feel I am missing anything by not retiring; I have travelled the world and had loving relationships throughout my life. I never married, never really wanted to, but had several significant men in my life over the years. My latest relationship is twenty-two years in duration and we both enjoy living separately, yet spending quality time together."

She plans to continue at her job, keep loving her partner, stay connected to her sister and family, and enjoy and have fun in life. Patricia McWade is an example of finding a full life while continuing to work at your chosen career vocation. Retirement for Pat is not in her future....at least, not yet.

NOTES

Patricia McWade, *Financing Graduate School: How to Get Money You Need for Your Graduate School Education*, Albany: Peterson's Publishing, 1992.

Bratter and Helen Dennis, *Project Renewment: The First Retirement Model for Career Women*. New York: Scribner, 2013.

Dean Patricia McWade at Georgetown

Intellectual Wellness

Volunteers Par Excellence

Maureen and Art Rosen

(Patricia)

> *"Nobody really knows how much anyone else is hurting. We*
> *could be standing next to someone who is completely broken*
> *and we'd never know. So, be kind always, with yourself, and*
> *others." –Anonymous*

> *"You can't be brave if you've only had wonderful things*
> *happen to you." –Mary Tyler Moore*

I met Maureen and Art when they moved to our subdivision on beautiful Lake Sunapee, New Hampshire. We'd finished building our dream vacation home three years earlier, and they had just built their retirement home. Maureen was 57 and Art was 65. Their youthful appearance and energy impressed me at the time. At age 42, I thought, "Hmmm....this retirement gig looks pretty good."

I watched as Art swam out to the mooring ball and brought the boat in to pick up Maureen, who carried a basket for a lake picnic with visiting children and grandchildren. I marveled at the lovely flowers that appeared on the association lakefront thanks to Maureen's gardening skills. Maureen and Art served on the association board as president and secretary, which included managing the septic systems for our association. They fondly referred to their committee as "The Effluence of the Affluent."

I just knew we'd become friends. When I asked about their history together, Maureen, a charming, blue-eyed, curly white-haired women, and Art, her professorial looking bespectacled husband, told me, "Eloping was the simplest thing to do 57 years ago when we married in a civil ceremony by the mayor of Yonkers."

Maureen came from a large Irish Catholic family in New Jersey, with no college money for girls. She said, "You became a nurse, a teacher, or a secretary. I opted for secretary and began working at an advertising agency in New York City at sixteen, while I was a senior in high school.

"My mother told me I should meet a college-educated husband at this fancy advertising firm, and that's exactly what I did. Art was a rising young advertising executive, Yale educated. But we had one big problem with my family—he was Jewish."

So this young couple's first struggle began. But love ruled, and they eloped. Art refers to their dating at the advertising firm as, "the great affair of the late 1950's, much like the TV show *Madmen*. Everyone smoked and consumed martinis at lunch. We called them silver bullets, but we were pretty useless in the afternoon."

Art's parents felt better about the marriage because Maureen agreed to raise the children in the Jewish faith. When her father suggested, "You could raise the boys Jewish and the girls Catholic," she drew the line. "No, Dad, I will not do that. And if you want to see your grandchildren you need to accept our marriage."

After a standoff, Maureen's mother talked to a benevolent priest who didn't damn them (as one priest had), but advised her to accept the marriage to keep peace and have contact with her grandchildren.

Maureen was 20 and Art 28 when they eloped. Maureen had to leave her job, but soon found another position in advertising. She left work with her first pregnancy to become a full time homemaker in Woodcliff Lake, New Jersey. They had three children in four years: two girls and then their son, Daniel Joshua. Life was good and they enjoyed raising the children in the Jewish faith. Art had served as president of the congregation in the past and Maureen became so involved she was asked to be President of the Sisterhood.

When Maureen told the rabbi she wasn't Jewish, he changed the temple's constitution to allow her to serve in this role. She said, "Oh well, why don't I just convert?" She did just that, and Art and she remarried in the temple with the three children by their sides.

Art informed me, "Maureen's opening remarks at her first address to some 400 attending congregants at high holiday services were, 'Temple Beth Or has had presidents who were doctors, presidents who were teachers, and presidents who were business people, but it's safe to say that Temple Beth Or of Washington Township has never had a president who was a graduate of Saint Cecilia's Academy of Englewood.'"

Art proudly went on to say, "If there was any tension about Maureen being president, it ended with that comment."

Art went off to work every day in New York City and achieved great success in advertising, earning the moniker "Mr. Excedrin" because he was account executive and interviewer of the on-camera Excedrin users. Maureen happily stayed at home raising the children, making her own curtains and creating a lovely home for her family. When her son entered high school, Maureen took a job as office manager for a busy real estate company. She eventually got a real estate license. Art proudly says, "She saved us $10,000 when we sold our house."

Around sixty years of age, Art started thinking about retirement. "We had enough money, and I was emotionally ready for a change. Our house was too big for us and we knew it was time to move. But move where? That was our next question. I thought moving was essential for our retirement."

"Why is that?" I asked.

Without hesitation, he said, "Changing your location is one of the biggest things for a successful retirement. I didn't want to see the young men going to work every day while I was out gardening. I knew it would make me feel out of things."

So he and Maureen put their heads together. They almost decided on Stuart, Florida, near his parents, but they discovered their second daughter was relocating to New England, where their oldest daughter already lived. Their son Daniel lived in New York City. Logic dictated a move to be near their children and grandchildren. Their son-in-law, who loved snow skiing and water skiing, suggested they look near Lake Sunapee, New Hampshire. And so the quest began.

They ended up at Blye Hill Landing, in Newbury, New Hampshire, and named their boat High on Blye, referring to their mountaintop home with a lake and incredible sunset views. Changing from suburban New York City to the mountains of New Hampshire was just what they needed and wanted for their "second life."

Art, who loves religious studies, says "I couldn't ask for a more different demographic from New Jersey, which was primarily

Jewish, Italian, or Irish Catholic, to New Hampshire, where we live among WASPs (White Anglo Saxon Protestants), Yankees, or French Canadians. Our move was like that old TV show *Green Acres*, where Eddie Albert sang, 'Green Acres is the place to be. Farm livin' is the life for me. Land spreadin' out so far and wide, Keep Manhattan, just give me that countryside.'"

Their "second careers" as volunteers began almost immediately at Lake Sunapee. Art started taking classes at nearby Dartmouth College at the Institute for Lifelong Education at Dartmouth (ILEAD), which later joined the network of Osher Lifelong Learning Institutes. He initially signed up for Chaucer's Canterbury Tales and Book of Exodus.

"After a few sessions, I told myself, 'I can do this!' I didn't mean I could take more courses; I meant I could teach classes."

History and western religion are his passions, and with power point skills and help from former secretary, Maureen, he created 15 courses for adult learning programs. He is currently teaching "ISIS: On the Road to Armageddon." Every course acknowledges Maureen as part of the team. A team they will always be. Art says, "It's not 50/50; it's really 100/100."

Maureen involved herself with Adventures in Learning at Colby-Sawyer College by doing all the photography and public relations while Arthur served as its president. The program prompted her to learn new skills as a photographer and graphic designer.

She said, "When I get bored, it's time to move on to something new." After nine years as a volunteer with Adventures in Learning, she began taking more photographs of the Lake Sunapee region. She became the Lady of the Lake and sold many photos on canvas. Photography became her avocation for years.

Then she moved on to volunteering to beautify Newbury with NBC (Newbury Beautification Committee) and was instrumental in renovating the Newbury Center Meeting House. I enjoyed presenting talks about my books at the Center Meeting House, with Maureen doing the advertising and public relations.

This dynamic couple kept their spiritual life alive and well by starting the Sunapee-Kearsarge Jewish Community, a fellowship group now in its fourteenth year. "The idea was Maureen's," Arthur appreciatively notes.

On the surface, it seems Maureen and Art led a perfect life. But we never really know what people are privately dealing with. While leading productive volunteer careers in New England they often worried about their son, who floundered in a film making career in NYC. Unlike his older sisters, who went into pragmatic, successful jobs as account executives, he chose the road less travelled—an artistic career in freelance film. Maureen and Art often financially subsidized Daniel throughout their retirement years.

After marrying and having a daughter, Daniel graduated from law school and passed the bar exam, hoping to create a more stable lifestyle for his family. But addictive tendencies lurked in the background, something Maureen and Art had worried about for years.

Daniel began using substances again and had an episode at a friend's house where he went berserk and the police were called. He checked himself into a rehab program. As Art says, "It was five weeks and thirty thousand dollars." He was advised to enter a halfway house, but returned to be with his wife and daughter. However, his wife asked him to move out.

Art and Maureen offered to let him live with them, but Daniel said he wanted to be near his two year old daughter, so they helped him find an apartment in New York City only blocks from his former home. It was only a short walk from the Brooklyn Civic Center where he hoped to find work as a staff attorney.

Everything seemed to be going well for Daniel, but the fateful call came one night in June, 2013. Their son was dead. He had overdosed when "huffing" Dust Off, an aerosol designed to clean computer keys. His addictions had taken their toll. He was gone.

Maureen remembers telling herself, "This is a critical juncture for our family. We must pull together now or it will destroy us." Her strength and wisdom at that time, along with the support of her husband and daughters, allowed their family to unite and survive. She said, "We went through all the stages of grief—anger, the guilt of 'what more could we have done,' the despair—but we knew we needed to be there for each other. We had to show our grandchildren how to carry on as a family. We let Daniel's wife know we loved her and wanted her and our granddaughter in our life. And so it has been. Every year we gather at Daniel's gravesite as a family to memorialize our son."

Maureen said, "I cried daily for a year and I still cry whenever I talk about Daniel. But I've met dozens of people with similar problems. Once you tell your story, people share with you. I'm often asked to help others who are struggling with a child's addiction or death." She adds, "You don't pass through this life without getting kicked in the ass at least once." Ain't that the truth!

Maureen and Art shared letters with me from Daniel's friends about their son. The sentiments in these letters help provide a soothing balm to their wounds and help them remember Daniel the person, not just his addictions.

And so this lovely aging, retired couple, Maureen and Art, continue living their volunteer lives, exploring all that life has to offer intellectually, emotionally, and spiritually, with an underlying chord of loss for their only son. Life goes on for their remaining children, their grandchildren, and the community they enrich with volunteer efforts. Thank you, Maureen and Art.

*Art and Maureen Rosen At Adventures
in Learning Dinner*　　　*The Young Rosens*

NOTES

Staying Engaged

As educator Nancy Schlossberg states in her book *Revitalizing Retirement*, it's important to get involved and stay engaged during retirement. "How do we combat the fear expressed when people say, 'I think I'm losing it?' The answer: Lifelong learning, a continuous process of learning new skills and acquiring new knowledge in a variety of formal and informal settings all through life."

Hundreds of schools throughout the country have set up lifelong learning institutes where courses are taught by university faculty members or people in the community who are knowledgeable and passionate about a topic. Learning and studying during retirement help keep our minds engaged and our thinking clear. As a bonus, we find new hobbies and meet new friends.

Many studies show that a healthy mix of physical and intellectual activity during retirement helps maintain overall wellbeing, decreases health problems, and eliminates such ailments as Parkinsons's and Alzheimer's disease.

For example, the Rush Memory and Aging Project, conducted in 2012 in Chicago with more than 1,200 elders participating, showed that increased cognitive activity in older adults slowed their decline in cognitive function and decreased their risk of mild cognitive impairment. The study showed that cognitively active seniors, whose average age was 80, were 2.6 times less likely to develop Alzheimer's disease and dementia than seniors with less cognitive activity.

Nancy K. Schlossber, Ed.D., *Revitalizing Retirement*, American Psychological Association, Washington, D.C., 2010. (page 37)

Crossing My Rubicon: Surviving the Loss of My Spouse

Chuck Hayward

(Patricia)

"We are all born for love. It is the principle of existence and its only end."
— Benjamin Israeli

"Irene and I never really thought of retirement."

That's how Chuck started his interview with me. Chuck's eyes sparkled as he spoke about his early years with the love of his life, yet sadness and weariness crept in as he relayed the last few years of Irene's life. Her failing health eventually led to their retirement as renowned tour guides.

He added, "Then I had a full time job in retirement of caring for the woman who made my life worthwhile." And that he did until Irene's passing on October 14, 2016.

Chuck says, "I didn't retire until Irene died because I was fully employed caring for Irene and had enough income so I didn't need to work."

At 85 years of age, Chuck began the journey of grief, and questioned what lay ahead for him. "Now that I'm alone I have to cut bait and fish."

I met Chuck a few months after Irene died when his physician daughter Kathryn, together with his two sons, Matthew and Jonathan, suggested he seek grief counseling. Baystate Visiting Nurse Association and Hospice directed him to my practice. Chuck and I felt an immediate connection; we share a love for words, art, and music. I guided him through the stages of grief and he renewed my education on the humanities and arts of life. Chuck is a man you can listen to for hours as one subject seamlessly flows into another topic.

Chuck has always been a teacher. He attended Pratt Institute and studied art on the GI Bill after serving the U.S. Air Force during the Korean War. He and Irene were married at the time and she worked as an RN at Massachusetts General Hospital to support the family while he attended college. After Chuck's graduation the family returned to the Connecticut Valley and he began teaching art for the Springfield Public Schools.

Chuck recalls, "I taught our State Representative Richard Neal, and the executive editor of the Springfield Republican, Wayne Phaneuf."

His influence stretches far and wide. During these years Chuck also taught studio classes at the George Walter Vincent Smith Art Museum, the principal art education institution in the Connecticut Valley. He continued graduate degree work and earned an MFAS from Boston University. After 11 years in the Springfield Public Schools he moved to Bay Path Junior College where he chaired the art department.

During his early years there, Chuck and Irene began escorting cultural tours. They started a business that continued for five years, called Hayward Cultural Tours, or as Chuck likes to say HCT: Help Chuck Travel. They were the "go to" tour couple for intellectual and cultured people in Western Massachusetts. Chuck jokingly remarks he knows the location of public facilities in most of the great museums on five continents.

Later, Chuck helped the Springfield Library and Museum Association dramatically expand their travel program. He joined Irene, who was already leading the expansive museum bus program, and together they led international and domestic tours for ten years, often in conjunction with other regional museums. Together, they organized and led over 100 passport trips and countless regional excursions.

Irene retired at age 70 for health reasons and Chuck remained with the museums until 2008 to train the new tour director, and complete a few more tours. At 78 years of age, Chuck hung up his professional tour guide hat, but he continued giving talks at the Springfield Quadrangle, a pro bono practice he started in 1971, on a myriad of cultural topics. Over time, he gave more lectures than anyone else in the association's history.

"My topics ranged from prehistoric cave art to Jackson Pollock. I gave many talks on two of my favorite masters: Vincent Van Gogh and Winslow Homer. My final Museums a la Carte Lecture was on March 31, 2016 and predictably the topic was: The Last Works of Vincent Van Gogh."

Chuck then became Irene's primary caregiver: "Full time nurse, cook, and bottle washer," as he puts it. In her last three years of life she underwent ten emergency hospitalizations. He never complained about this, but accepted their new roles as the ending part of an exceptional and unique life journey with his Irene. After her last hospitalization in October, 2016, she came home under hospice care. Shortly thereafter, with family and friends singing and talking to her, Irene peacefully passed.

"We opened champagne at that time and celebrated her life," Chuck says. A month later a public Memorial Tribute was held at the D'Amour Art Museum to honor Irene Hayward. This became the largest attended public event in Quadrangle history.

Chuck says, "The initial gut wrenching pain I felt during the months after Irene died felt like more than I could stand." But, as we talked in therapy and I explained the process of grieving, Chuck began healing and stepped into his next chapter in retirement as a widower.

"What I don't like about being alone are all those white days in my calendar where nothing is planned," he told me. Keeping the dance card full is one of his goals right now. He knows many people, but isn't a traditional group joiner. He does not see himself in a "barracks community," which is how he refers to some retirement communities, or living in Florida. Although he travelled the world, he never worked more than eight miles from the town where he was born.

He says, "Everything I value is within a day's drive of my home."

Now, with Irene gone, Chuck continues the journey alone. Many times he mentioned he'd like to fall in love again, but wonders if that's possible at 86 years of age.

He says, "If it's not to love, what are we here for?"

I ponder this and agree.

The research of George Vaillant, study director of the Harvard Study of Adult Development, concludes that love is the most important factor for flourishing in old age. Vaillant found that love in adulthood can modify the traumas of early life.

Chuck says, "There's much to enjoy and learn in life, but without love, life would be too thin of purpose for me."

He continues enjoying a full intellectual life, has great friendships, and keeps himself as fit as he can. Chuck can still wear the white dress sport coat he wore on his first date with Irene in 1954. Unbeknownst to Chuck, Irene kept this coat throughout their 62 years of marriage. He wore this coat (size 42R he proudly states) to Irene's memorial service.

That kind of love and team-ship may be difficult to find again, but Chuck wants to stay open to the possibility.

He's keenly aware of aging: His back aches and he finds it more difficult to work on his precious bonsai trees in the backyard. But Chuck continues swimming and working out almost every day at the health center where he meets some of his cohorts for chats. He also plans lunch and dinner engagements with new friends, and with a network he and Irene developed over the years when they ran the travel programs.

"What advice do you have for future retirees?" I asked.

"Find ways to celebrate your journey. Almost every day I try to share the most meaningful lessons I learned from our travels. For the future, I think people should actively embrace any irksome issues that come up. Look at aging as a gift. Seek solutions to these issues through intelligence, persistence, and patience. As Yogi Berra reminded us: 'It's not over till it's over.'"

As we speak about his plans for the future, Chuck says in a reflective minute, "My Rubicon will come."

"What exactly does that mean?" I ask.

In his kind, professorial way he explains that an 1875 painting by Adolphe Yvon, entitled "Caesar" portrays Julius Caesar crossing the Rubicon River in 49 BC. He adds, "That event led to the Roman civil war and ultimately to Caesar becoming dictator for life and the rise of imperial Rome. It changed the course of Caesar's life."

Chuck's version of crossing the Rubicon is considerably less dramatic than Yvon's grand portrayal, but like Caesar, he hopes to find a course of action that will add continued meaning to his life.

Chuck recently wrote me that his daughter says he continues "living in a box." And he wonders when—and where—he will find a key that leads to the next stage of life.

As he completes the first year of grieving after the death of his beloved Irene, I wish for Chuck love, opportunities to share his wisdom, and the blessing of finding true companionship. I believe Chuck's "wellness" in this phase of retirement will depend on his emotional and social connections.

Chuck and Irene Hayward

NOTES

George Vaillant, *Triumphs of Experience: The men of the Harvard grant study*, Harvard University Press, Cambridge, MA., Pg. 61 (2012).

Accepting Yourself is Part of Getting Old

Barbara Bernard

(Helene)

> *"A graceful and honorable old age is the childhood of immortality."* —*Pindar*

I thought of Barbara Bernard some weeks ago when I read the New York Times July 30, 2017, article titled "Life among the Boldfaced Names" by John Leland. In his article Leland describes the current life of 94 year old Liz Smith, a well-known tabloid gossip columnist who died in 2017, at home.

You may recall Liz Smith as a sophisticated woman who hobnobbed with the rich and powerful and made stars of wannabes. The interview revealed that after having a stroke Ms. Smith lived alone, depended on a walker, and rarely left her Manhattan apartment. At one point in Leland's interview she stated "I am in search of Liz Smith. After a lifetime of fun and excitement and money, feeling important, and being in the thick of it, I am shocked every day that I am not the same person. I think that happens to all old people. They're searching for a glimmer of what they call the real self. They're boring, mostly."

When I read that passage I felt sadness and pity for Liz Smith. And I thought of Barbara Bernard, who exemplifies the opposite viewpoint.

Barbara and George Bernard remained active in the Holyoke and Springfield, Massachusetts social scene for years. George died at 75 after a happy 50 year marriage. Despite financial challenges, Barbara described a solid marriage in which her husband always encouraged her to do what she wanted. When their manufacturing business struggled for years, Barbara was pleased to have her own successful career in journalism.

When asked about her successful marriage, she said, "Both of us always tried to leave work problems at the door when we came home."

Barbara's interest in journalism developed during high school in North Adams, Massachusetts and continued at Mt. Holyoke College. She began with radio work and transitioned to television after marrying George. In both venues she produced her own shows and promoted women's programming. She was the first woman in Western Massachusetts to have her own television show and interviewed many famous people.

She said, "I especially remember being a contestant on the New York City radio show "Strike it Rich" in 1950. With the $100.00 prize money I organized the Holyoke Golden Age Club, which was the first independent organization for retired men and women in the nation. I was only 23 years old at the time."

Over the years Barbara served on the board of directors of countless organizations, chaired fund drives, and won national and local awards for broadcasting and journalistic accomplishments and community service. Among other things, she was honored for recording 2,000 books for people with impaired vision and helping found and support several theatre groups.

Barbara recently celebrated her 90th birthday with 300 of her closest friends. An article by Cynthia Simison, managing editor of the Springfield Republican, where Barbara has worked as a columnist for years, describes her as "a good friend and mentor." Ms. Simison goes on to say Barbara "rarely acts her age" and described her daily swims at the YWCA.

Barbara swims about five days a week after rising at 4:30 in the morning. Accepting her physical limitations, she enters the pool with a lift to help fight the bone on bone pain of arthritis in both knees. Speaking of knee replacement surgery, she said, "I don't have many years left and I don't want to waste the time it takes to have surgery and rehab. I can still manage to stay at home with the help of three walkers placed around the house. I even learned to go down stairs backwards. I've learned to adapt."

After successfully battling two bouts of cancer, Barbara isn't about to succumb to arthritic knees. She declined entreaties from her two out of state daughters to live closer to them, saying, "If I moved, they would be the only people I knew."

Friends are a vital part of Barbara's life and she's a regular visitor at local hospitals and nursing homes. The timing of our telephone interview depended on when her friend would be released from the hospital after surgery. Barbara transported her friend to the hospital early that morning and would bring her home as well.

Barbara stays active with her senior center, yoga, symphony concerts, local theaters, and movies. When out and about she graciously greets everyone she knows (generally half the audience) with her warm smile and kind eyes. She has an uncanny ability to recall names and details of people's lives. She still calls my husband by his boyhood nickname and shared many social activities with my mother-in-law who died ten years ago.

Sometimes she feels like "the last man standing," after attending so many funerals for friends and colleagues. She said, "I still feel close to my friends' children. These young friends reassure me that life goes on."

After a 70 year career in journalism Barbara continues writing a weekly newspaper commentary on world, local, and personal events. She maintains a sense of humility and graciousness toward everyone. Ms. Simison's article describing her 90th birthday celebration pointed out that Barbara helped break the glass ceiling for women on TV news. At the gala event she basked in the accolades of current and former television colleagues and said,

"This is a chance to see what my funeral might be like—only I get to be here!"

In 2009, Barbara became the first woman to receive the Valley Press Club's Lifetime Achievement Award. Described as a true pioneer in the broadcasting industry, Barbara humbly referred to herself as "lucky." I believe a lot more than luck was involved in her success, including spunk, intelligence, faith, perseverance, kindness, grit, humility, and a sincere love for people.

When we look at Barbara's long, full life, every element from the eight dimensions of wellness is present: physical, emotional, social, spiritual, occupational, intellectual, creative, and financial. Not surprisingly, she has strong opinions about retirement:

"I never thought about it."

Nor does she intend to stop writing. "I will write my own obituary. I enjoy putting thoughts down. I think retirement can be a disaster if you love your work; maybe not so much if you hate it."

"Do you have one piece of advice for people approaching the traditional retirement age?" I asked.

She quickly responded, "Don't retire! Maybe don't keep the same job, but everyone needs a purpose, something to do. The worst move is to stop doing things. I love being busy, accomplishing projects, and being rewarded for it."

She added, "Of course we older people need to accept some slowing down and changes in appearance. Getting older is a time to relish and reflect on life's accomplishments. Accepting yourself is part of getting old."

If only Liz Smith had had the opportunity to know Barbara and learn from her wisdom.

Barbara Bernard with Great Grandchildren

When a Terminal Illness Forces Retirement
Jim Madigan
(Patricia)

> *"I love those who can smile in trouble, who can gather strength from distress, and grow brave by reflection. 'Tis the business of little minds to shrink, but they whose heart is firm, and whose conscience approves their conduct, will pursue their principles unto death."* Leonardo da Vinci

> *"Even death is not to be feared by one who has lived wisely."* Buddha

I've known Jim Madigan for over 27 years as WGBY Public Television's voice of Western Massachusetts, where he moderated the local show "Connecting Point" and a weekly talk show called "The State We're In." Jim interviewed me on multiple occasions to discuss psychology topics, talk about my books, and provide a psychologist's perspective on political panels. I always enjoyed being on the air with this two time Emmy award winning journalist. In 2017, Jim announced he was leaving the station because of a terminal lung disease called idiopathic pulmonary fibrosis. After being diagnosed with the disease in 2015, he managed to continue working for two years by reducing his hours.

He said, "WGBY was great about letting me work part time and do research at home. I continued working as long as I could because I loved it. But the time came when I realized even a half hour interview exhausted me. Breathing became tough and fatiguing. I also found it harder to drive to and from work. I knew it was time."

Jim grew up in upstate New York, the only son of an only son. He adds, "And I have an only son, Jim IV. My mother and father were always interested and active in politics in Schenectady, New York. My Mom loved FDR, and it was a requirement that my Dad be a Democrat if he wanted to marry her. My mother Ruth's grave marker reads, 'Beloved wife, mother and Democrat.'"

Jim adds, "It's no wonder I became interested in politics at an early age. I attended Mount St. Mary's College in Maryland and studied History and English. Mom advised me not to go to schools in DC for fear I would cut classes to attend political events—probably a wise suggestion."

Jim began his career as an aide for a New York state senator. "Although I loved politics, radio and TV fascinated me. I remember watching David Brinkley in 1956 cover the national presidential convention and thought I'd love that job."

And so he began working at radio stations in New York until 1979, when he moved to Westfield, Massachusetts as news director at WLDM, which later became WNNZ. He worked there for three years before becoming a general assignment and politics reporter for ABC Channel 40 in Springfield, Massachusetts.

In 1990 Jim joined public television and PBS station WGBY hosting the local public affairs series, "Page 57" and producing "The State We're In," a weekly segment focusing on regional, state and national politics. Jim also partnered with the Springfield Public Forum to interview national and international authors.

In a Springfield Republican article announcing his retirement, Jim related, "One guest I'll always remember was Doris Kearns Goodwin who came on the show and talked about her books on Lincoln and Lyndon Johnson. I also had the opportunity to sit down with Paul Rusesabagina, who inspired the film 'Hotel Rwanda.' Such a fascinating man. It was a gift to meet him and interview him."

In 2012, Jim won praise for his straight-forward style moderating a pivotal debate between U.S. Senate candidates Scott Brown and Elizabeth Warren that was broadcast nationally by C-SPAN.

As I interviewed Jim at his home, his wife Lena of 34 years would poke her head in the door to make sure he was okay. She lovingly reminded Jim to sip his drink. On several occasions when Jim had coughing spells, Lena would be right there by his side. I could see they were a loving, devoted couple. Jim made sure to tell me, "I am blessed to have her in my life."

When we began discussing Jim's decision to retire, Lena joined us to share her feelings about having Jim at home full-time. She said, We never discussed retirement before his diagnosis. After that, everything changed. We agreed Jim should work as long as possible, but retire before he could no longer do the job well.

"As his breathing became more and more labored and fatigue set in, we decided together it was time to 'go out.'"

Jim added, I never pictured myself retired. I wondered what I'd do. When I took time off in the past I read newspapers or tuned in to radio and TV political shows, so I relaxed by doing what I did when I worked. I had no idea what else to do.

"Quitting at age 65 wasn't a decision I would have chosen to make, but it became necessary. However, I was surprised how relieved I felt after releasing the tension of coordinating work projects. I no longer went to bed, or woke up, thinking about who I'd be interviewing. I don't miss the stress I sometimes felt because I wanted to be prepared and do my job to the best of my ability."

"What have you found to do in retirement?" I asked.

Jim smiled and said, "I'm reading the books I always said I'd read someday—mostly history. And I probably watch more news TV than is good for my health, given the current political scene in our country."

The struggles of retiring for Jim included coping with his terminal disease. Hospice was involved and a nurse came twice a week to check on him. Lena was relieved to know she had someone on call.

Jim said, "I used to worry about getting dementia like some members of my family, so I'm relieved to know I won't die that way."

He made a comment I've heard from some of my clients, "It's rather surprising to me, but there's tremendous peace in knowing how you're going to die. We all die sometime, so I find relief in knowing how I'll go." Lena teared up when she heard this.

Lena works as an office manager for a husband and wife law practice. "They're very flexible with my time and I go in two days a week now. They know I'll take more time off as Jim's health declines."

"Do you have any advice for other people in your situation," I asked Lena.

She wisely said, "Do what you can when you can. Live each day to the fullest. Don't sweat the small stuff. Be grateful for the little things. I now realize how much we enjoy just being together, reading the newspaper or watching TV. Enjoy what you have."

Lena and Jim touched hands at that point. They both said almost in unison, "We're just happy to have each other."

Throughout this ordeal Lena and Jim maintained a sense of humor. When Jim's diagnosis was made, Lena remembers telling Jim, "I guess I really do take your breath away." They both laughed as she said this.

I marveled at the peacefulness this couple reached. Jim knew difficult days lay ahead, and he planned to spend them in simple everyday activities with his wife, his son Jim Madigan IV, and his rescue Shih Tzu named Jefferson Adams.

Regarding the dog's name, Jim jokingly said, "I felt like Hamilton was getting a lot of attention, and I'm fascinated by Thomas Jefferson and John Adams."

Always the political historian, I thought.

Thank you, Jim, for sharing your wonderful career and courage as you faced your terminal illness. Although not a retirement he would have planned, Jim and Lena faced the future together with love, faith and courage.

NOTES

With great sadness I relay that Jim passed away on Saturday, May 26, 2018, just three weeks after I finished his chapter. Tony Dunne, the executive producer of "Connecting Point" summarized him perfectly.

"Jim was a true gentleman, unparalleled in his political knowledge and his ability to distill that knowledge to the viewer. His like will never be seen again, I think. His human approach to reporting is something I think is desperately needed and will be greatly missed in our current political discourse."

And I add: He was just a really nice guy. We will miss you, Jim.

Jim Madigan with Friend   *Jim Madigan's Show "The State We're In"*

Creative Wellness

From Subaru to Shakespeare
Will Cooke
(Patricia)

> *"Polonius: This above all: to thine own self be true. And it*
> *must follow, as the night the day, thou canst not then be false*
> *to any man. Farewell, my blessing season this in thee."*
> *William Shakespeare, Hamlet, Act 1, scene 3.*

Our career paths sometimes take sudden turns and uphill struggles we never anticipate and didn't choose. Such was the case with Will Cooke, born in upstate New York as the oldest of six children. In 1919, Will's grandfather had begun a long automotive career as a salesman with the first Ford dealership in the area. Will's father followed suit many years later when he purchased the Cadillac/Oldsmobile dealership in Ithaca, NY, where Will and his family moved when he was sixteen years of age.

Life was good, with Dad building a business and Mom at home raising three boys and three girls. Will's mother was a talented musician and singer who fostered the artistic side of each child and made sure music was part of their lives.

Will's father worked diligently to grow the business, yet encouraged the children to follow their own passions and dreams. Will went off to Georgetown University where he began as a pre-med student. After a year of struggling with organic chemistry and calculus he switched to an English/Philosophy track. Upon graduation he decided to become an attorney and returned home to Ithaca after graduation with plans to begin law school in September. However, when he saw his father, Will realized his plans had to change. He could see his father was dying, while everyone else continued with life as though his dad would recover. Although sadly aware of the danger presented by the diagnosis of late stage colon cancer, the family maintained the intense belief and hope that Dad would beat it. Perhaps because Will was the oldest son, he knew differently. He scrapped his plans for law school.

The inevitable happened in December 1973, when his father died at 46 years of age, leaving a widow and six children. As the oldest son, with a college degree, Will felt a responsibility to care for the family. His pledge at the time: "I have to support this family and make sure each of my siblings gets the same opportunity I did to go to college." His mother had never managed household finances, being busy raising six children. At 21 years of age, Will became the man of the house.

Will's father was an only child, and his paternal grandparents were in their seventies, living in Rochester. His grandfather, retired after 40 years in the car business, "came off the bench" at age 73. He and Grandma moved to Ithaca to help Will manage the car dealership and protect the family. Will immediately completed two "crash courses" (Northwood Institute and GM Institute) to learn about running a car business. He had to prove he was capable of becoming his father's successor before GM would approve him as dealer/operator. At the time he was the youngest "unofficial car dealer" in the United States at age twenty-one.

To make matters worse, the auto industry was in terrible straits through much of the 1970s. Few remember the awful impact of the oil crisis; big gas guzzling cars were not selling. Crippling interest rates of up to 20% slowed the economy to a standstill. This wasn't a good time to be in the car business. And to make things more difficult, GM was actively seeking another, more experienced dealer to purchase the dealership.

Will and his grandfather knew the market for autos was at its lowest ebb since WWII. A sale then would yield only pennies on the dollar—not adequate to support Will's mother and the other five children. So Will and Grandfather persevered and within three years Will had proven himself to GM and became the official agency dealer.

Will speaks candidly, saying, "I was never a car guy. But I learned to sell cars and manage the business, partly because I felt a responsibility for the employees. I turned out to be a fairly good businessman and bought other car dealerships along the way. I made a good living to care for my mother and send every one of my siblings to college. I had a good life, but being a car dealer was never *me*. Cars were just inventory to me; a means to an end to support my family."

He attributes his ability to "make it work" to the discipline he learned while rowing crew at Georgetown. Getting up at 5 AM in the freezing cold and rowing for two or three hours builds tenacity and grit. And I needed that grit to keep on going in those early, challenging years of responsibility for the business.

"When I thought the last tuition bill was paid, my youngest brother (after years of applying) was finally accepted to veterinary school. So my duty as eldest son continued." He went on to say, Although being a car dealer was never my dream career, it felt gratifying for several reasons. The money was rewarding and by this time I had a wife, two daughters, and a son. I also enjoyed being a community leader and employing 140 people in the Ithaca area. I stayed involved in community service through many institutions, including the United Way and Catholic Charities of Tompkins/ Tioga Counties. I especially enjoyed mentoring young people to become better technicians, sales people, or whatever career they chose.

The time came in the 1990s when I began planning to sell our seven franchises. None of my five siblings or my three children wanted to take over the business. My major responsibilities to family were behind me, so at age 56 I was ready to move on. After years working with a broker who brought in 'high rollers' from across the country to buy the business, in the end we sold to the local Ford dealer down the street. He had what I didn't: several adult children anxious to enter the automotive industry. So my career as a car dealer from 1973 to 2008 ended at last.

After 35 intense years running the car business, at last Will could follow his true passion. He and his wife Carol, his Georgetown college sweetheart, began assessing if and where they might want to move. They were tired of Ithaca winters and wanted a place with intellectual stimulation and an interesting urban style of living. They decided to return to Washington, D.C., where they both enjoyed student life at Georgetown, and where their two daughters were finishing college.

Carol, who had worked in Admissions and Development at Cornell University, segued seamlessly into volunteer work for

Georgetown University Admissions and Development. Will, on the other hand, hoped to pursue his passion in music and theater. He applied to and auditioned for admission to the prestigious MFA program of the Shakespeare Theatre Company's Academy for Classical Acting at George Washington University. He was pleased to be accepted into the class of 16 students, most of them younger and in mid-career as actors. He was the oldest in age and the least experienced class member.

During the intense one year program he learned stage combat, dance, speech, yoga and Pilates, but with strong emphasis on "all Shakespeare, all the time" scene work. Classes were physically and emotionally demanding. He almost walked out at one point when the assignment required "digging around in the cellar of your psyche." He jokingly said he was startled to learn this sort of training "required having a nervous breakdown." But once again Will persevered, saying: "To hell with this, I'm not going to quit."

He told himself, "Four years of rowing at Georgetown and thirty-five years of combat as an auto dealer prepared me for anything. I can stick this out, too!" And he did.

Will's courage to take this calculated risk is recommended in the book by Roger Landry, M.D., *Live Long, Die Short*. "Taking calculated risks, taking risks where the potential outcome is growth, joy, increased competence, and reduced risk of decline is acceptable, even recommended, risk. In fact, I strongly recommend to my presentation audiences that they do something that scares them every day.... It must take you out of your comfort zone. Remember, *we cannot grow if we don't change*." (pg.144).

Will has been in at least one play a year since grad school, with performances at the Shakespeare Theatre Company, American Shakespeare Center, the Baltimore Shakespeare Festival, the Folger Theatre, the Studio Theatre, and several theaters in Virginia and Maryland. He played Henry II in "The Lion in Winter" with the VpStart Crow Theatre Company. His directors include Tony Award-winning Michael Mayer and Helen Hayes Award winners David Muse and Michael Kahn.

During this second career Will flourished playing kings, dukes, and judges. At 6 feet 5 inches, with silver hair and piercing blue eyes, he's often the tallest—and oldest—actor on stage. He has done over 2500 voice overs for business and public service commercials and performed in more than 40 plays.

Before his full-time stage career, Will kept his sanity as a car dealer in Ithaca by performing at Cornell University with the Cornell Savoyards and at the Hangar Theatre, where he acted in a handful of plays and several Gilbert and Sullivan operettas while making life-long friends. He would often leave work at the car dealership and rush off to auditions or rehearsals. (His grandfather, no patron of the arts, would have questioned this, had he known.) But Will knew this creative outlet was crucial to both his professional and personal life.

"What do you like best about this unusual form of retirement—a new career?" I asked.

He replied. "I'm happy to no longer be stressed by and responsible for 140 employees. But sometimes I do wonder if my life today has sufficient purpose. What am I doing to earn my heartbeats? Acting is fun, creative, and fulfilling, but I have down periods without work. Sometimes I feel I could use a rudder. I don't want to just take up space."

Even after ten years of retirement, Will is still figuring it out at age 66. He feels he needs a little more structure in his life to feel productive.

Will often comments on how lucky he's been in life. He says, "That's a genuine reflection of how I feel, given the help I received from my wife, grandfather, and countless others. But the coin has another side I may not have emphasized enough. I find myself not only thanking the good Lord for my happy circumstances, but also asking His assistance to help me balance the scales with service—in whatever form that may take—to justify my good fortune."

He added, "I've been only partially successful in this effort. But I'm still young enough to have another go at it. I'm thinking about volunteering a few mornings a week with an organization called 'So Others May Eat,' and at one or two other nonprofit groups."

"What advice do you have for other retirees?" I asked.

"Be a little cautious about a new life that's suddenly free of stress and structure. And be careful about alcohol." Will says that after retiring from the dealership he saw himself drinking more during the week than at any time in his professional life. He didn't like it, so committed to "one and done" in any given situation. This is good advice for future retirees. Be aware, monitor yourself, and seek help if you need it.

Will is a testament to following your creative passion, no matter what age, as an avocation or a vocation. Will's final words of wisdom regarding retirement are:

"To thine own self be true."

He goes on to say, "You know best what works for you and what you need, so listen to your heart. It's good to consult people you trust—your spouse, financial advisors, lawyers, and the like. But ultimately the decisions are up to you. You must decide if retirement is for you or if you want to continue working. Listen to yourself."

Will Cooke

NOTES

Roger Landry, M.D., *Live Long, Die Short*. Greenleaf Book Group Press, Austin. Texas, 2014.

Reclaiming the Operatic Voice

Deborah Houston

(Helene)

> *"If music be the food of love, play on."*
> William Shakespeare, Twelfth Night

Deborah was born performing, it seems. Her tutu enhanced pirouettes from age three are still available on vintage home movies. Today she'd be a star on YouTube, Facebook, and even America's Funniest Videos.

From the beginning Deborah's mother and maternal grandmother encouraged and supported her vocal talent by introducing her to opera through recordings and the Saturday broadcasts of the Metropolitan Opera Company. Her mother, an excellent pianist, helped Deborah prepare for solo opportunities in church and school. When Deborah turned 18 she began taking voice lessons and continued solo work with her prep school glee club, receiving her school's music award when she graduated. She first attended Westminster Choir College and then Hartt School of Music at the University of Hartford, seeking her Bachelor of Music Degree.

When Deborah arrived at Hartt, the vocal department head told her she would concentrate for two years on reworking her vocal technique to develop her full potential. Therefore, no lead roles in the school operas would be open to her. She could only participate in the chorus. This news devastated Deborah at first, and also shook her confidence. But it was truly a blessing, because Dr. Elmer Nagy, the Hartt Opera Department director used scenes and soliloquies from Shakespeare's plays to teach acting technique to singers. He recognized her acting ability and helped her develop into the classically trained actor she is today.

Meanwhile, Deborah's vocal technique steadily improved. At the end of her junior year when she and her classmates took individual vocal exams adjudicated by two Metropolitan Opera stars, Deborah received high marks for both the art song and opera aria she performed. But more importantly, the Met artists generously shared their concerns that her beautiful voice was hampered by a physical obstruction. They referred her to a medical specialist. Surgery to correct a deviated septum opened up her instrument in a way no vocal technique, however fine, could do.

While at Hartt, Deborah not only honed her acting skills, but also her finesse as a costumer. She uncovered this talent while participating in a work study program to assist professional costumers of the opera department. As a child she created elaborate costumes for her little sister and neighborhood friends from a costume box filled with old clothes, evening wear, and fabric. Those skills, coupled with the training in sewing and costume history she received as a child from her mother and grandmother, would not be wasted.

Following graduation, Deborah's voice and acting talent (aided by her ingénue good looks) helped her land acting gigs in summer stock and dinner theatre. Two years later, remembering Dr. Elmer Nagy's advice that she go to England to continue her classical vocal and acting training, Deborah traveled to London, where she was accepted by The Guildhall School of Music and Drama.

Deborah had the good fortune to supplement her Guildhall studies by taking private lessons with three faculty members from the Royal Academy of Dramatic Arts. She also studied and became certified in armed and unarmed combat for the stage. Fortunately she still found time to explore London and travel on semester breaks with friends to other parts of England and Europe. Her love for English and European history, from the Middle Ages through the 18ᵗʰ century—with special attention to the Renaissance and Shakespeare—melded with her abilities to set the trajectory of her career.

When she returned to the states and moved to New York City, Deborah, found a day job to pay her expenses while networking, auditioning, and performing in independent productions throughout the city. Finally, in 1980, Deborah auditioned for and was invited to join the Jean Cocteau Repertory Company. There she played many challenging roles in rep. Both her singing and acting in the dual roles of Thaisa and Marina for the company's production of Shakespeare's *Pericles* brought her critical acclaim in the New York Times.

In 1983, Deborah founded and became artistic director of Kings County Shakespeare Company in Brooklyn, a company that would earn an impressive 25-year history. The company showcased her talents as actor, director, dramaturge, costume designer, and occasionally as a singer, but her beloved opera arias and art song were temporarily set aside. Regularly reviewed by the New York Times, the company performed in different indoor and outdoor venues, most notably the 1500 seat Prospect Park Bandshell and at the Brooklyn Academy of Music. For twelve years during this time Deborah also managed to teach voice and speech in the Saturday School of The American Academy of Dramatic Arts. And, as an adjunct professor, she taught classical acting and Shakespeare at St. Francis College where the company was in residence for four years.

Deborah spent 35 years of her adult life in a Brooklyn Heights studio apartment where every square inch holds heirlooms and memorabilia. She also worked for many years as an office receptionist, earning enough money to be independent, have health insurance, and acquire a pension. These necessities can make an artist's life stressful. Finding a paying job that gives the flexibility to pursue an artist's primary career is no easy task. In order to keep up with the demands of her multi-faceted schedule, Deborah always protected her health with regular check-ups, screenings, and much attention to diet and exercise. Her flexibility, energy, and strength put many younger associates to shame.

Since childhood Deborah has had a strong and abiding faith. She is a genuine seeker of the truth and the light. She became enamored with the Anglican Church while in England and was introduced to St. Michael's Episcopal Church on the Upper West Side of Manhattan. She says, "That long subway ride to church from my home in Brooklyn is well worth the effort. It's a progressive church filled with theater and music professionals, so I feel very much at home."

Deborah cultivates a strong social network through the church. The friends she made at church, and later through her theater company, are remarkably supportive of each other and generous with sharing their time and contacts. Deborah never married despite several long term relationships, but her friendships offer support in what can be a cold urban environment.

At age 60, as the economy and politics made solvency more and more difficult for her company, Deborah decided to retire from her role as artistic director. She decided to become an independent contractor, focused on her directing and costuming skills. During her mid-60's the law firm where she worked as front desk receptionist dissolved and closed its doors forever, leaving Deborah without a steady job. She had planned to do office work at least until age 70.

At this point Deborah's skill at living on a shoestring budget paid off. She decided the loss of her job could be a blessing in disguise and (even at her age!) allow her to fully pursue her art. Now self-employed, she works with various acting and opera companies and schools as a director, teacher, and costumer. Her work with a local opera company rekindled her love of singing opera and she began studying with a voice teacher for the first time in many years. Her current teacher sings with major opera companies and has brought Deborah's voice to a whole new level.

Deborah had an epiphany during a trip to the Holy Land while she was in Caesarea Maritima, Israel, a former playground for the ancient Romans built by King Herod. An ancient amphitheater overlooking the Mediterranean Sea is renowned for acoustical design that amplifies sound throughout the enormous theater. The pastor/tour guide knew of Deborah's vocal talents and, without warning, asked if she would sing on that ancient stage to demonstrate how the sound traveled.

Without hesitation or the ghost of self-doubt that dogged her singing during her first three years at Hartt, Deborah strode to the center of the stage and proceeded to sing acapella Mozart's beautiful aria *Ave Verum Corpus*, flawlessly and with great poise. The music was heard above the crashing waves of the Mediterranean below. Strangers in the amphitheater stopped talking and all eyes focused on Deborah.

From that moment, Deborah in her retirement has enjoyed a new lease on life by singing the classical music she loves, fine tuning it, and sharing it with others.

She says, "I want to make sure I don't leave this life with unsung music still inside me."

Deborah today at the
Metropolitan Opera in NYC

The P.I.P.'S "Previously Important People" Retire

Ron and Pat Pantello

(Patricia)

> *"There are only two ways to live your life. One is as though nothing is a miracle; the other is as though everything is a miracle."* —Albert Einstein

I met Ron and Pat while vacationing with friends in Sarasota, Florida when this dynamic couple invited my husband and me to join them for a boat ride around the local inlets. During the ride we shared information about ourselves—careers, families, and interests. As usual when I'm involved with writing a book, I asked them about my current topic du jour, which in this case was retirement.

When I mentioned retirement to Ron and Pat, I felt like I'd hit the jackpot on a slot machine. As coins of wisdom kept pouring out, I knew they had a great story to tell for *Well-Come to Retirement*.

Ron spoke candidly about how entering retirement eight years earlier was difficult for him. He said over lunch, "I've been called a PIP by my children."

"What does that mean?" I asked.

"A Previously Important Person," Ron answered.

A lightbulb went off in my head. He was the type of person often described in retirement books—one who struggles with adjustment because his former work was a large part of his identity. In her book, *Revitalizing Retirement*, Dr. Nancy Schlossberg writes, "After retirement, some people still yearn for their former role, power, or prestige. They have not given up the need to be on center stage. That is understandable; when you've been at the top, you feel entitled to maintain your position as a leader and winner." (Pg. 91).

To my delight, Ron and Pat wholeheartedly agreed to share their story for the book. They are a power couple who struggled, yet forged on to find peace and happiness in retirement. Plus, they're both delightfully funny. Let me introduce you to Ron and Pat:

Ron describes his parents as polar opposites. "Dad was the son of Greek immigrants, fun-loving and adored by anyone he touched. Mom was a Southern belle and a stern moralist. That must have been a great romance!"

Ron's humor continues as he describes his military career starting at age six when he was sent to military school because his parents were busy running two drugstores in Georgia. When his parents moved to Florida they had him come home and attend the public school system, ending his military career at the ripe age of eleven. Ron was an only child until age sixteen when his sister was born; his father served as a mentor throughout his life.

Ron attended college on a football scholarship and transferred to a school closer to home when his mom became terminally ill with cancer. After graduation his dad arranged interviews with pharmaceutical companies, and thus began a stellar career that went from sales, to marketing, and then to advertising for healthcare communications companies. In New York City, Ron was CEO of Euro RSCG Life network, a worldwide advertising agency.

He says, "I wandered into advertising somewhat by accident. My intention was to stay in Manhattan for only a couple of years, adding a paragraph to my resume. But I found my passion. Let's say the rest is history. Lucky me."

In contrast to her husband, Patrice (Pat) says, "I grew up in a loud, funny, Irish-Catholic family on Long Island. My two older brothers and I were expected to prioritize schoolwork. For our parents, a grade of C was equivalent to an F. We had many nuns and priests in our family and I always attended Catholic schools. Once, for fun, the nuns dressed me in their garb which made for a very cranky five year old. My parents expected all their children to attend college and fully supported us along the way."

After attending Marist College in Poughkeepsie, NY, Pat started her first job in New York as an editorial assistant at *Better Homes & Gardens*. "I worked hard and was rewarded with promotions and generous raises each year. My career moved so fast that when my boss said 'We need to talk,' I actually thought he planned to fire me. Instead, my meager salary doubled and they gave me an office and an assistant."

At twenty-nine Pat was recruited by Doubleday. She said, "I was swept into the world of best-selling fiction, glitzy parties, colorful celebrity authors, and extravagant book rights' auctions. I felt I had arrived, but a few years later when another firm bought our company, I found myself without a job."

Never one to give up, Pat joined a project with her then-husband and a team of other PhD's who were beginning an "image study" on behalf of the NY Stock Exchange. Pat relates, I was fascinated by the project and realized consulting was dynamic. After that project I set up my own subsidiary rights firm representing publishers' rights to non-traditional markets. I happily grew that business and every day seemed exhilarating until 9/11, when my head and my heart seemed to fracture.

"Many of my clients and friends suffered losses on 9/11. Unexpectedly, my untreated PTSD came to the surface and depression brought me to a standstill. Instead of eating, sleeping or working, I was crying and shaking uncontrollably."

Pat goes on, "It took a few years of excellent therapy and good doctors to improve my health and direction. Suddenly, I realized I'd inadvertently slid into retirement!"

Pat and Ron met in 1981. She said, "There seemed to be a spark between us, but we were both married at the time. When we reconnected in 1995, we knew we were meant to be.

In 1998 Ron surprised me with a wonderful birthday party at Milo's in NYC. The guests were childhood friends, my brother and cousins, college roommates, and even my precious step-children from my former marriage. In the middle of the party Ron made a toast and proposed marriage. Everyone in the room—thirty of my favorite people in the world—were in on the plan, except the waitress and me. I was so startled I started to cry and couldn't answer right away.

"When the waitress asked me, 'Is this for real?' and I sputtered and said I didn't know. We were married a year later in the garden of I Trulli's restaurant with my former husband's daughter and Ron's sons as our witnesses. Ron's cousin from Georgia officiated and it was perfection."

When I asked Ron about retirement he said the two of them already knew where they wanted to live—Sarasota, where an age-friendly community focuses on the needs of retirees. But Ron goes on, "Timing was another issue. Sometimes events we can't control decide the exact timing to end a career. In my case, yet another merger by financial activists motivated me to retire because my goals differed from the new owners' goals and I no longer needed the money.

"Financial independence doesn't make you happy in itself, but it does give you the flexibility to maintain your integrity."

Pat added, "When Ron finally retired he seemed like a man without a plan. This was a huge adjustment for him, since work consumed his head and heart for so many decades. I kept busy volunteering and taking classes, but those weren't good options for Ron."

She went on to say, "I manipulated the situation a bit by making 'adult play dates' behind Ron's back."

Ron agreed. "I felt a bit lost at the beginning of retirement; so much that my wife began making play dates behind my back...Ha!"

Within a year Ron found interesting activities to pursue. "Creativity was always part of my life so I tried writing screenplays, with a little success. This evolved into writing stage plays, which are much easier to get produced, at least locally and regionally. Ultimately this became my passion and keeps me off major medication."

Many of Ron's plays were performed in theatre competitions in the Sarasota area and include such titles as *Sons, Mothers and Others*, and *I'm Dead When I Say I'm Dead*.

"What do you like most about retirement now that you've settled in?" I asked Ron.

"I can sum it up in one word: Independence—the freedom to do whatever we choose. No pressure, no schedule, but plenty of time for our creative endeavors."

Pat said, "I love waking up gently without an alarm. For too many years I got up at 5:30 in the morning for a two hour commute, each way. That was brutal. Now it's a treat to feel rested. On a more serious note, I'm devoted to volunteering with meaningful causes, such as education, conservation, and women's issues. It's a joy to learn, engage, and pick and choose challenging areas of focus—for fun."

"What other advice do you have for retirees?" I asked.

Ron said, "Hang around with positive, fun friends and be available to them; they can become your second family. Don't waste time on the negative; it takes too much energy. And protect yourself from emotional vampires who are petty, judgmental, unsafe, or just plain mean."

Pat went on to say, "Be grateful—you're blessed to be alive. Be gentle with yourself and embrace your good fortune. Take your cues from older friends who enjoy good health and, more importantly, good attitudes. Keep your body and mind in motion and remember to make every precious day better than the last!"

Ron added, "The most important thing in retirement for

Pat and Ron Pantello

me is having a great spouse. That's probably the most vital part of a happy retirement. Work at that relationship every day."

I thank Ron and Pat for sharing their retirement story and hope their joy continues with many creative and fulfilling years ahead. And Ron, I'm waiting for an invitation to opening night for one of your plays!

NOTES

Age-Friendly Communities

In her book *Too Young to Be Old*, Nancy Schlossberg writes about Sarasota, Florida, the state's first age-friendly community. To welcome retirees Sarasota focuses on transportation, housing, social life, convenient outdoor spaces and public buildings, civic participation and employment, respect and social inclusion, and community support and health services.

To find out how a particular community rates on AARP's Livability Index, complete their tool online at http://www.aarp.org/livabilityindex

Schlossberg recommends during the retirement transition that one must be patient. "Let go of the past, search for the future, then create your new life." *Retire Smart, Retire Happy*, pg. 25. Be patient, give yourself time to adjust to the retirement transition.

Nancy K. Schlossberg, Ed.D., *Too Young to Be Old*, American Psychological Association, Washington, D.C., 2017.

Living for Art

Rosemary Tracy Woods

(Helene)

> *"You use a glass mirror to see your face; you use works of art*
> *to see your soul."*
> George Bernard Shaw

As the only sister of eight brothers, Rosemary Tracy Woods was always a standout in her family. One brother happened to be Harold Melvin of Harold Melvin and the Blue Notes. While growing up in Wilmington, North Carolina with her grandparents, living in Philadelphia with her mother and stepfather, or working for her brother, she said, "I was always a rebel who set my own course in life."

When I asked what made her a rebel, she recalled being reluctant to accompany her aunt to her job as governess to a wealthy family. The child Tracy said, "I ain't gonna polish some white people's silver." Instead, she slipped off to her favorite refuge, the Philadelphia Art Museum, where her interest in African American art took root.

Thus the journey began...living for art.

Tracy has a beautiful face with large, expressive black eyes. I can only imagine how appealing this art-loving child must have been. Love for art continued throughout her life and finally reached fruition in the nonprofit Art for the Soul gallery in Springfield, Massachusetts, where Tracy is executive director. The gallery promotes diverse artists from around the world and the exhibits, programs, and activities illustrate historical, political, and social passages through the present day. Tracy charges no admission and provides a venue for artists who haven't been able to exhibit in mainstream settings. She doesn't hesitate to address sensitive topics like racism and white privilege.

Working on the campaign of Edward William Brooke III, the first African American to be elected to the US Senate helped stir Tracy's political activism. Tracy's first job with the State of Connecticut was interim director for the Governor's Committee on Employment of Persons with Disabilities, under the appointment of Lowell Weicker. In this position she was charged with ensuring all state agencies adhered to the new Americans with Disabilities Act.

Moving from that position to Administrative Assistant for the Director of Affirmative Action, her office ensured minority contractors were included in all set aside programs. These positions caused her personal dedication to advocacy to kick in.

"I learned to speak out," she said. And she has never stopped

In 2010, Tracy accepted the Unsung Heroine Award from the Massachusetts Commission on the Status of Women. Her work also caught the attention of then Governor Deval Patrick. But all the accolades in the world don't put food on the table or prevent disappointment, tragic losses, and ill health. Tracy pointed out to me that her generation didn't receive the same information as whites regarding such things as retirement plans and 401 K's. That situation changed as financial advisors and other groups placed a higher standard on informing all women about long term goals, regardless of their race.

Tracy said, "Fortunately I always believed in saving and getting financial counseling, which helped me survive in my older years."

She now owns Art for the Soul gallery and launched her own arts consultant business, RTWoods Arts.

Earning a master's degree in Arts Management and Museum Studies was a lifelong goal for Tracy, but the degree doesn't seem as important today as it did several years ago. Tracy says she'll continue to travel, take various courses that interest her, and keep advocating for people who can't advocate for themselves.

Thank you so much, Tracy, for sharing your remarkable story with us.

Tracy Wood Celebrates Heritage

Financial Wellness

The Crone's Rebellion

Elaine Frankonis

(Patricia)

> *"Creative people are curious, flexible, persistent, and*
> *independent with a tremendous spirit of adventure and a*
> *love of play." —Henri Matisse*

During our lives, sometimes creative wellness and fun seem more important than planning and financial preparedness. Such is the case with Elaine, who describes herself as always being something of a rebel. Coming of age during the 1960s fueled her wild streak.

Elaine grew up in Yonkers, New York above the funeral home her father directed. The first in her family to attend college, she had no real passion for study, but maintains, "I just wanted to get out."

Secretary, teacher, or nursing were the choices for women back in 1958. Becoming a teacher seemed the safest bet for someone who loved to write, as Elaine did. She met her husband in college and they eloped when she became pregnant during graduate school. As a young couple they both worked in the college bookstore and then her husband became a high school English teacher in the small rural community. As her husband wrote plays, Elaine wrote poetry.

Elaine remembers, I felt trapped in the role of wife and mother. By then it was the 60s and the feminist movement had started. The first issue *Ms. Magazine* changed my life. I knew I wasn't alone— that other women struggled with the same issues. My husband and I were probably too much alike. Two creative people vying for attention wasn't good.

When he told me I was fourth on the list in importance to him, behind his job, kids, and art, then I knew we needed to divorce.

"After that I was a single mother raising two kids, but resourceful and a good networker. I first landed a job at a local college writing grant proposals, then transferred to the NY State Education Department where I worked for 20 years with a fantastic female boss. This was an exciting place to work. I coordinated dozens of cultural and artistic projects. I loved it!"

Even while raising her two children, Elaine said, "I enjoyed life before retirement because I knew how to have fun and we had an active singles organization in the Albany, New York area with weekend dances and week-night programs. I had all the socializing with friends I wanted."

Elaine says she lived paycheck to paycheck while raising her two children. Although she wasn't a planner, she knew she'd have her state pension and Social Security. She thought that income would be enough for retirement.

But circumstances often detour our funds elsewhere. Elaine's mother showed signs of dementia and was living with Elaine's uncle in Yonkers—a widow and widower. When her uncle's health also deteriorated, Elaine became the live-in caregiver for her mother.

Although Elaine's daughter moved on and married, her son continually hopped from one odd job to another and depended on Elaine for support. Finally, at age 48, he was diagnosed on the Autistic Spectrum with Aspergers Syndrome. Elaine initiated the diagnosis and helped her son find employment through state services. But throughout most of his life she paid for his housing from her social security check.

Elaine's retirement at 60 years of age wasn't planned, but came about due to her mother's health. She cared for her mom for five years, and spent the next five years sharing caregiver responsibilities with her brother.

She says, "That was a difficult and lonely time for me." From 60 to 70 years of age she moved away from her social network to care for her mother and support her son. "After I retired and moved away, I left my social life behind. Later I had to find a way to start over and figure out how to reconnect with the social fun I used to have. Well, maybe not the same kind, but reasonable substitutes."

After her mother died Elaine decided to enjoy life again. Finally, it was her turn! At age 70, Elaine felt ready to start a new phase of retirement. She'd always been close to her daughter, son-in-law, and grandson, so with money from her mother's estate Elaine built an addition onto her daughter's house for her "retirement pad."

She said, "It took me a year to decompress." She pointed to a swing in her front yard. "That's where I would sit to swing and read. I was happy and began to shift gears."

After a year or so living with her daughter's family, Elaine realized she needed more social life. She said, Retirement might be easier for folks in a relationship. For single people like me, loneliness and isolation are big challenges unless you're part of a larger community where you can socialize.

"Every situation is different, and mine was difficult because I moved away to live with my daughter and family and didn't know anyone in the area. I'm not a church-goer, and senior centers didn't inspire me at all. Compounding that were the physical results of aging: bad night vision (for driving), arthritis, and knee problems. I could no longer do many of the things I used to do for fun. But the hobbies and interests I developed over the years sustained me and eventually gave me ways to meet new people."

As a psychologist I've often heard this complaint from people in their 70's. I began to term the phase Three Quarter Life Crisis. At around 75 many people find their physical bodies don't cooperate in enjoying the lives they once lived. This is a time when people must search deep to find other creative outlets. Such was the case with Elaine. But she "put on her thinking cap" and came up with wonderful substitutes for fun and stimulation in her seventh decade of life.

According to Dr. Stuart Brown, author of *Play: How It Shapes the Brain, Opens the Imagination, and Invigorates the Soul*, play is "spontaneous and allows for improvisation." He says our society is so work oriented that people often neglect to incorporate play into their lives. He also believes play is vital for a happy retirement. Elaine and many other people agree with the importance of fun and play in retirement.

Elaine was one of the first women in her age group to start a blog. Given her feminist political nature, Elaine's blog is about national and international issues. Entitled "Join the Crone's Rebellion," you can visit the blog at www.kalilily.net. (Kali is a Hindu goddess of strength and motherly love, full of fierce energy and power).

Elaine found writing the blog empowering; she credits it with saving her sanity and allowing her to connect with other blog writers and express her confrontational personality. She started the blog in 2001 while caring for her mother during the isolated time in her life, and continued it through the move to her daughter's home.

In 2008 Elaine was asked to participate in a seminar at Harvard University with other bloggers which she found inspiring. Elaine was quoted in a Wall Street Journal article from June 14, 2008 entitled "Put it in Writing."

"I blog to connect with the world outside myself
that I'm trying to make sense of. I blog to keep up my spirit;
to stir the spirit of others; to stir my blood, my brain, and my beliefs."

But the blog was virtual reality and Elaine needed more contact with real people, so she started a writer's group at her library. There she met like-minded, interesting people.

Elaine loved ballroom dancing, but painful knees stopped that hobby until she discovered gel injections that relieved the pain. She searched and found a dance group in a local Polish community, where she now enjoys weekly polka dancing on Sunday afternoons. She can drive to this event because it's in the day time. Elaine has also found a local senior center with interesting theater productions. She is in her first play in retirement and loves the camaraderie with other actors.

As Elaine explores her creativity and need for socialization in retirement, she finds her networking skills come in handy. She no longer feels the same pull toward political activism, but now looks for fun ways to engage in creative political activities. She makes T-shirts that express political and book themes. I often wear one of her "bookshirt" creations when I give book talks for my book *Liars, Cheats, and Creeps* about relationship abuse and violence.

Elaine continues writing poetry and recently had one of her poems published in *The Peregrine Journal*.

"What advice do you have for other retirees?" I asked Elaine.

"Money becomes more important during retirement and life as an elder can be stressful if you don't plan for the financial end of things. Life can throw major challenges at us. Unfortunately, I've never been a long-term planner; fortunately, I knew I could count on a decent pension from my state government job. Unfortunately, the cost of family issues put a real dent in the income I live on. Plan for the worst and hope for the best. I guess that's good advice for any endeavor."

She continues, "Fun is so important. I found one of the best ways to plan a great retirement is to develop interests and hobbies during your working life that you can continue when you no longer spend your days at a job. Creative outlets in any art form—painting, writing, theater, quilting, knitting—keep your mind busy and your spirit vital."

Elaine's vitality and energy is a force to be reckoned with. Like the Hindu goddess Kali, she perseveres and is a force of time. Kali is the goddess who liberates souls from the cycle of birth and death, constantly reinventing herself. A quote from Elaine's Kalilily.net blog site sums it up:

> *Every culture honors its version of the Crone.*
> *She is revered as a cornerstone of her community –*
> *as a healer, comforting with herbs and words;*
> *as a fierce champion of the oppressed.*
> *as a repository of the wisdom of her tribe.*
> *Those who fear her, call her "witch."*
> *Those who love her, call her Grandmother.*

Elaine Frankonis

NOTES

Stuart Brown, *Play: How it Shapes the Brain, Opens the Imagination, and Invigorates the Soul*, NY, NY, Penguin, 2009.

Patricia Peters Martin, Ph.D. and Renee Forte, *Liars, Cheats, and Creeps: Leaving the Sociopath Behind*. NorLightsPress, IN., 2016.

Unexpectedly (and Unintentionally) Independent

Gail Fei

(Helene)

> *"Someone's sitting in the shade today because someone*
> *planted a tree a long time ago."*
> *Warren Buffett*

The clouds part and the sun comes out when Gail enters a room. Her short blond hair is her trademark and her merry blue eyes and ear to ear grin immediately put everyone at ease. At times her diction and bawdy humor reflect her humble beginnings (one of 13 children), but don't be fooled. This is an accomplished musician, educator, and doctoral level college professor of education.

Four years ago Gail lost her dear husband of over 50 years to acute myeloid leukemia. They had a fulfilling marriage based on four credos: Faith, Fun, Family, and Financial Planning. Horst was a retired police officer who lived for and loved his profession. Known for being kind and fair to all, Horst was a common sight in the community with his fit physique, doing bicycle patrols. He was all about healthy living, so his sudden illness came as a shock to everyone, especially Horst himself.

Gail said, "I took copious notes of everything that happened in his illness: all his medications, appointments, and reactions. I have a thick file because I knew he was going to beat this. He would defy the odds because he was so strong and had such a healthy heart. I wanted to document all of it for the book I would write about how he defeated the odds."

Horst came to the United States from Germany at age 11. He couldn't speak a word of English and schools didn't accommodate immigrants at that time, so a Polish immigrant student taught him English while the class was going on. In high school he was a popular jock with the nickname Virgin Ears because of his lifelong dislike of swearing. He and Gail met when he was a senior and she was 16. They remained a couple for the rest of his life, much to the chagrin of the popular high school girls who were shocked at his choice of a not-so- well-known underclassman.

Gail's mother instilled great faith in her. Each Sunday they walked together to the nearby Congregational church. She was the self-described pet of her father, the youngest girl of 13 children. Gail believes the close relationship with him was probably related to her near death at age two from spinal meningitis.

After her marriage Gail wanted to become a teacher and Horst worked three jobs so she could attend Hartt School of Music for a degree in music education. For 15 years she integrated special needs students into the elementary school music program and spent 17 more years teaching kindergarten. Along with her career, Gail had two daughters and remained active in her new church, right around the corner.

She later earned a doctorate and taught math and language arts for the elementary school in three area colleges toward the end of her teaching career. Few people are aware she is Dr. Fei.

She said, "I don't believe in boasting about myself. It used to embarrass me when Horst bragged about me. He was always so proud."

Gail has been retired for 14 years now, if you can call it that. She and Horst bought a Florida condo in 2001, which she still enjoys while splitting her time up north between the family home where her daughter now lives and the lake cottage in the Berkshires she and Horst bought in the 1980s. She continues to play the piano and organ for special events in her church in Massachusetts and serves as organist in her Florida church from September to March each year. Her appointment book explodes with commitments when she returns to Florida. She's an active volunteer, donating treasure and talent, and creating musical events for the retirement community she calls home.

Horst enjoyed boating when they visited the lake house and Florida. Gail said, "I went out with him on the boats because it made him happy. I sailed with him for 50 years; I don't need to do it ever again."

She feels pretty much the same about marriage. "I had such a fulfilling marriage, nothing could replace it or compare." So all the men in Florida whose heads turn in her direction when she enters a room might as well look another direction.

Financial foresight is one of the greatest legacies Horst gave his daughters and Gail. "He was always conscious of retirement. When he worked nights he listened to radio talk shows and learned the ins and outs of saving and the need to have everything in place. So he started a vigorous savings plan at a young age."

She added, "Horst wanted to not only survive, but enjoy retirement. He made wise real estate decisions that protected and benefitted our family."

While Horst had a positive, hopeful outlook toward retirement and a few years to enjoy it, Gail didn't like to think about retiring. "I loved what I was doing," she said.

When Horst died, Gail had six months of acute grief and would become overwhelmed with sadness. About the fourth month after he died, a close friend gave her a book that helped her gradually come to terms with his absence and her life ahead.

Mark Nepo's *The Book of Awakening: Having the Life You Want by Being Present to the Life You Have* includes passages of comfort that reframe loss and give hope and direction. Gail often reread these sections of the book. She poignantly recalled some of Horst's heart breaking last days spent in the family home.

She admitted to feeling some relief when his pain ended. "I couldn't be selfish and try to delay his departure."

During his illness, for ten months she and Horst rose at 4:30 a.m. to drive from western Massachusetts to Dana Farber Institute several times a week. She said they were "playfully in love" all through their relationship. One of the last times they drove back from Boston, after hearing there were no more trials or treatments to help him, Elvis Presley's song "Love Me Tender" played on the radio and she saw Horst was weeping. He knew his life would soon be over.

"But," she adds, "everything made him happy. He was born with a bucket list and fulfilled it all. He had no regrets."

Now, four years after Horst's passing, Gail can say, "You have to play the hand you're given. Don't waste time with regrets. That isn't useful."

Giving to others is what Gail finds important. We're all here to help others. I always think about what purpose I might have, so I donate food and money to help others in need.

"Horst was the head of the household, but now I'm in charge and I kind of enjoy that. I'm less concerned about what other people think and I value myself more. Feeling more secure in my decisions is freeing, and empowering."

Horst is still present in Gail's life. His name comes up frequently in conversation and often the memories are punctuated with laughter. He remains a vivid presence in the family home. Upon entering the living room you first see a beautiful cherry wood baby grand piano. "Horst always said that was his first boat," Gail says with a laugh. A large framed photo of Horst hangs on the opposite wall. He looks healthy and strong with his familiar grin, bending over a newly cut Christmas tree."

Gail revealed a recent event to me: "I don't believe in a lot of the supernatural stuff you read about, but something happened. Horst and I selected his grave site shortly before he died. He chose a spot in the town cemetery within walking distance of our home and close to the main street of the town he loved and protected for years."

Gail said she recently went to the site and washed the stone, with special care to his photo imbedded in the granite. Next to the stone sits a metallic pinwheel their grandson Marco put in the earth following a Pentecost Sunday service. She said, "Just as I finished working the pinwheel began madly spinning without the slightest breeze. I think the moving pinwheel was a sign of approval from Horst—a welcome sign."

Gail's story is one of lifelong love and the importance of faith, family, and giving back. Her life also provides an example of how careful planning, saving, and wise investing softened the blow of unexpected loss. Horst must be at peace knowing the love of his life is comfortable and living the life he planned for her.

Gail Fei and Horst

Gail Fei at the Organ

Establishing Financial Wellness
(Helene)

In the previous story Horst and Gail teach many lessons about financial wellness.

Horst was always learning: He listened to every financial expert he encountered, even as a young man. Such experts can point out sound investments that enable your savings to grow and support you during retirement.

Horst and Gail were conscientious savers: They took advantage of 401K savings plans as soon as they could.

Horst and Gail invested in real estate that not only grew in value, but also enhanced their lives. The family home, now shared with their daughter's family, allowed Gail to maintain close friendships in her church and community. The summer place on the lake is a destination spot for the family, yet gives Gail and her local daughter privacy during the summer months. Their daughter who lives in Georgia is grateful for the lake house. The Florida condo Gail and Horst purchased was not only an excellent investment, but gave them a new social community to enjoy—a group of people who provide support for Gail in her independent life.

Horst was a planner who looked forward to an enjoyable retirement. In order to have this, it's important to figure in advance about your living expenses and whether your plans are realistic. Learning to budget early in life is an important skill for a satisfying retirement when you live on a fixed income. Both Gail and Horst worked long enough to qualify for full retirement income through pensions and social security. Other people, after analyzing how much retirement will cost, sometimes delay their retirements, continue working part time, convert home equity into savings, move to a less expensive area, pay off debt, and eliminate unnecessary expenses.

Horst couldn't be duped: As a law enforcement officer he could smell a rat easily as marijuana smoke from a car window. However, many seniors are vulnerable to financial fraud and scammers become more creative all the time.

Avoiding Fraud

My father was a victim of fraud while in his 90's and I still feel like crying when I think of how this former businessman and informed investor stepped into a clever trap. His situation was described in a 2016 Forbes Magazine article titled "Why Older Adults are so Susceptible to Financial Fraud."

Scammers realize many older people struggle with their finances and feel sad because they have nothing to leave their relatives. Then someone calls and says, "Congratulations! You just won a huge prize!" My vulnerable dad believed the caller, which left the door open for endless mail encouraging him to send money in order to get his prizes—fantastic claims of health and financial security.

Studies show senior citizens are more trusting than younger people because of actual changes in the aging brain. Executive function becomes compromised, affecting judgment and analytic abilities. Activity decreases in the part of the brain supporting important "gut feelings" that alert us to danger and untrustworthy people. Aging and changes to the brain can result in a perfect storm for fraud—becoming overly trusting of others while, at the same time, feeling overly confident about our ability to handle finances. Older adults, family members, and financial advisors should work together to recognize these risk factors and avoid fraud.

A 2016 study done by True Link Financial revealed that adults age 60 or older lose $36.5 billion dollars each year to financial fraud. Much of this money goes to schemes such as grandparent scams, home improvement scams, and IRS scams. Con artists target older adults who may have savings accounts and be isolated, lonely, or cognitively impaired.

Resources;

DaDalt, Olivia, "Why Older Adults are so Susceptible to Financial Fraud." Forbes.com, December 18, 2016. https://www. forbes.com/sites/nextavenue/2016/12/18/why-older-adults-are-so-susceptible-to-financial-fraud/

The National Council on Aging has an excellent webpage detailing the top ten financial scams targeting seniors: https://www. ncoa.org/economic-security/money-management/scams-security/ top-10-scams-targeting-seniors/

The MIT Age Lab offers tips, resources, and research to help prevent seniors from falling victim to financial abuse: http://agelab. mit.edu/resources-help-protect-older-adults-financial-fraud-and-abuse

The Benefits of Saving for a Rainy Day

Doug

(Patricia)

"Financial peace isn't the acquisition of stuff. It's learning to live on less than you make, so you can give money back and have money to invest. You can't win until you do this."
Dave Ramsey

Doug is an example of someone who practiced fiscal responsibility from the day he began working. Being a disciplined saver early in life made a huge difference for him.

Doug grew up in a predominantly Italian neighborhood of Springfield, Massachusetts, the third of four sons to working class parents. His father, whose World War II nickname was Ace, always worked at least two jobs, with his primary career as a machinist in a factory. Doug describes his mother Louise as the household CEO/CFO, and she also worked as a bookkeeper. He greatly admired the work ethic of both parents and believes their example inspired him to become a good financial planner and committed worker. His mother was in charge of the family finances, reading the Wall Street Journal regularly and following the stock market. Her investment acumen permitted his parents to retire at 60 years of age and live comfortably until their death in their late 80's and 90's.

My parents were raised during the Great Depression, and as a result they instilled strong fiscal discipline in each of us children. Throughout my life they preached about fulfilling wants and managing needs as well as learning to make do with less. My mother often spoke of saving for a rainy day.

"Thanks to their fine example I began planning for retirement as soon as I started working in 1973."

When Doug was 16 a tragic car accident killed his older brother. This devastating event shaped Doug's future life in that he became his parent's emotional caretaker. The tragic incident also left Doug with a keen sense of responsibility and self-preservation for his physical safety. The death occurred midway in Doug's senior year at high school. After that, he no longer felt committed to college and his major in education. He left college after six months to begin work in a factory.

He said, "My father's heart was broken by this, because he didn't want any of his sons to follow his difficult career as a factory worker. But I needed to find my own way. After a year of factory work I knew that wasn't the life I wanted. I enrolled in the police academy in 1973."

And thus began Doug's 43-year career in the criminal justice system. He took advantage of the Federal Law Enforcement Assistance Act under which he could earn a bachelor's degree in criminal justice and a master's degree in criminal law.

As he approached 14 years of service as a police officer, Doug's sense of self-preservation kicked in and he looked at administrative positions in the state's court system as a magistrate in the district court. He finished earning a second master's in Public Administration and attended the Institute of Court Management at the National Center for State Courts, which enhanced his career opportunities in the state judicial system.

Doug enjoyed his role in the court system and continued as magistrate for 29 years, retiring after a total of 43 years in the state's criminal justice system. He aggressively invested, planned well, and had a comfortable retirement at 63 years of age.

But, as much as we plan, life does take twists and turns. In Doug's case that involved meeting Patti, his soul mate, at 49 years of age and having their first child at age 51. Doug had been married at a younger age, but didn't have children from this first marriage. During his extended marital separation and divorce he led a single life style without responsibilities beyond caring for himself. When he met Patti she had an 11-year-old son, Ryan, from a previous marriage. (Ryan has since graduated from college and is employed). Doug and Patti decided they wanted a child together.

At the start of their marriage Patti and Doug both worked 60-hour weeks, built and furnished their new home, had a baby, and cared for Doug's aging parents who were about to move in with them.

"No stress at all, right?" I asked Doug.

"It was crazy for a while," Doug agreed. "Good thing we met later in life when we'd achieved our academic goals and were well positioned professionally and financially." He added, "Patti is more free spirited than I am and her spontaneity is a good balance for me."

Even though Doug had a long standing financial advisor and was an avid follower of financial publications by Kiplinger and Ramsey, he still had concerns as retirement age approached. He crunched the numbers over and over, routinely consulted with his advisors, and often discussed their finances with Patti. Everything seemed fine, yet he still felt hesitant.

Doug realized this uneasiness was twofold, "One, would I be okay financially, and two, how would I manage the change from my professional identity to being the household CFO and stay-at-home Dad?"

With reassurance from Patti and their advisors, Doug decided to retire a little over a year ago. He now says, "Here's the big surprise about my retirement: How amazing it is! Being away from the stress of my job and the structured environment is indescribable. I love everything about retirement. The freedom to be in charge of every single day allows me to make life a little better each day for my family. Now I have a chance to pursue my interests and hobbies as I choose and at my own pace. After working for forty-five years in law enforcement, the change in pace and lack of daily structure is unbelievably rewarding."

Doug's health improved after retirement. His blood pressure significantly decreased, as did his antihypertensive medication dosage. He's able to work out regularly, enjoys cooking interesting meals for his family, and he loves that he can read on a daily basis. In his first year or so of retirement he read over forty books simply for pleasure.

Doug relates with tears in his eyes, "I now have the joy of spending time with our son Billy every day, watching his independence and intellectual curiosity develop. Each morning I stroll with him to the end of our driveway as he prepares to walk to school. I hug him and tell him I love him before he leaves. Partway down the walkway, when Billy turns and waves at me, I see a reflection of myself. It's almost as if I'm watching myself grow up all over again."

"What advice do you have for future retirees?" I asked Doug.

It's important to develop a strong sense of fiscal responsibility at an early age: Acquire the skills to budget, tell the difference between needs and wants, and be sure to save and invest money.

"My mantra has always been to pay yourself first, before any other financial obligations. By being a disciplined saver early in life you take advantage of money compounding over the years, which is excellent for retirement planning. I recommend you invest aggressively in the stock market in order to create personal wealth. And I stress the importance of getting competent fiscal guidance at an early age when you start crafting your retirement plan. I engaged a financial advisor thirty-five years ago and I'm so glad I did. That guidance was invaluable for planning a successful retirement."

Doug and Patti's next stage of retirement is scheduled to start in five years when Patti retires. Their son Billy will head off to college and they'll begin their third phase together as they explore retirement as a couple living on Cape Cod, a lifelong dream for Doug. Thanks to careful financial planning and hard work, they will continue having a comfortable, satisfying, and positive retirement experience.

NOTES

Is it Too Late for Me?

Not everyone reaches retirement age in solid financial condition. Things go awry for various reasons including lack of planning, illness, family issues, unexpected job loss, and financial setbacks. The future can seem terrifying without a plan. But getting a late start doesn't mean you have to give up on your retirement dreams.

For late-comers to retirement planning, the Internet, AARP, government agencies, and books offer helpful ideas. For example, an online article by *Forbes Magazine* offers eight ways to start saving for retirement after age 50. These ideas include reframing your thinking to get past fear, looking for ways to generate more income besides savings, and revamping your retirement plans.

An article by AARP encourages seniors by saying, "Working a Bit Longer Could Pay Off." The author believes delaying retirement even for a few months is a more effective way to boost your living standard as a retiree than bumping up your late-career savings. Even a small amount helps, because it's a starting point.

References

Chandler, Dahna M. "8 Ways to Start Saving for Retirement After 50," Forbes. October 19, 2017. https://www.forbes.com/sites/

nextavenue/2017/10/19/8-ways-to-start-saving-for-retirement-after-50/#2fae6ecb3092

Mannes, George, "Working a Bit Longer Could Pay Off," AARP, January 30, 2018. https://www.aarp.org/retirement/retirement-savings/info-2018/delay-retirement-fd.html

Physical Wellness

Maintaining Physical Wellness as We Age
(Helene)

> *"He who has health, has hope; and he who has hope has*
> *everything." — Thomas Carlyle*

Having a satisfying retirement, or Third Act, is nearly impossible without good health. Too many retired or older adults exhaust themselves going from one doctor's appointment to another, week after week. These appointments can become our main focus and social life, as health issues sap our strength and spirit. Although not all health issues can be avoided, being proactive about health issues can help prevent many unpleasant surprises.

For example, everyone should know the health histories of their immediate family members, because inherited genetic traits for illness often run in families.

Helene's Experience

My mother suffered from painful, crippling osteoporosis and arthritis and had a broken hip at age 66. Knowing this, I began having bone density screenings in my mid-forties and eventually took a bisphosphonate that treats bone loss and helps prevent fractures. So far I've experienced no fractures. My bone density improved and has stabilized for several years, even off the medication.

I inherited high cholesterol from both parents, so I never balked at taking statin drugs that help control my blood lipids and prevent cardiovascular disease. My mother had a poorly functioning thyroid gland which she refused to treat, and that probably contributed to her chronic depression. Her sister also had low thyroid levels. For many years I've taken medication for my hypothyroid condition and have the levels monitored as needed.

I inherited my father's redhead complexion and propensity for sun damage, in my case worsened by years of sun worship. So every six month I have a check-up with my dermatologist. I see the eye doctor regularly to monitor pressure in my eyes, since glaucoma is common to all my maternal relatives and I don't want to jeopardize my precious eye sight. My mother's sight was compromised by both glaucoma and a stroke. She didn't want to take a blood thinner after having a TIA (transient ischemic attack) and in her late 70's she had a stroke related to atrial fibrillation. Her damaged eyesight broke my heart, because reading was her greatest pleasure.

My mother's experiences confirmed what I already knew as a nurse about the importance of regular health screenings, staying informed about family history, and taking advantage of the latest developments in treatment. Along with helping you stay fit, these practices may also lengthen your life and help you to feel more in control of your destiny.

Finding a primary care provider who works as a health partner and cheerleader is essential, and we all deserve that. If you aren't so lucky, keep looking. Some years back I worked with a patient who had complex medical and psychiatric issues. She took a mood stabilizer that caused a movement disorder. Her primary care physician took time to call me and talk about his concerns. His voice reflected warm feelings for this patient as he presented the issues as a collaborating colleague, not an accusatory superior.

After the call I told myself, "I wish I had a doctor like that," followed by the thought, "I can have a doctor like that!" I proceeded to transfer my own healthcare to his practice.

If you aren't able to advocate for your own healthcare, find someone who will. Take a relative or a friend with you for important appointments and ask that person to take notes, remind you of things, ask questions, and lend a second set of ears. When we feel anxious it's hard to process what's being said. Come to appointments with a list of questions and don't leave until they've been answered. Learn to speak up; your providers are not mind readers.

I learned a shocking fact a few years ago: When a prescription of any sort is written, 1/3 of patients will take the medication as prescribed, 1/3 will not take the medicine exactly as prescribed (eg. take it once rather than twice a day), and 1/3 of patients will never take the medication at all. If you aren't taking a medication, tell the prescriber. He or she can then make adjustments to your healthcare plan. Don't be shy about explaining your reluctance and concerns.

My mother's lifelong aversion to taking medications (despite nurse's training) did not bode well for her. In her last years when she suffered greatly from multiple illnesses, she developed a pill taking ritual. At the end of a meal she would open her little pill case, hold the pills in the palm of her left hand, and gaze at them. I still wonder what she was thinking. Was she sad at having to give in to the medication, feeling defeated, like she lost the battle? Now I'll never know, which makes me sad. When I take my medications I feel empowered. I know they're helping me.

Living Up to My Potential

Walter Glover

(Helene)

> *"The purpose of life is not to be happy. It is to be useful, to*
> *be honorable, to be compassionate, to have it make some*
> *difference that you have lived and lived well."*
> *–Ralph Waldo Emerson*

Walter Glover is unique: a man with purpose, passion, laser focus, and an incredible inner voice. Recently I was privileged to interview this 70 year old self-described "flatlander" from Indiana. Everything I read about Walter prepared me for how unusual he is. At age 50, after an award-winning career in journalism and 20 years in hospital administration, Wally changed course to study theology and become a hospital chaplain for the next 15 years.

At age 59, while reading about Mt. Everest, Wally heard a voice say, "You can do that." After realizing the voice wasn't going to leave him alone, this rookie mountaineer trained for nine months and accomplished the difficult trek and climb to Mount Everest Base Camp at 17,600 feet in Nepal. Despite suffering acute mountain sickness, Wally's success in Nepal led him to dream of climbing the Seven Summits, the highest mountains on each of the seven continents.

He felt inspired to use the treks as fundraisers for fighting childhood obesity through a charity he founded, 2Trek4Kids. By climbing mountains around the world he raised $135,000 for three rural St. Vincent Hospitals in southern Indiana to establish youth weight management clinics and give scholarships to hundreds of youth through the clinical programs. Later he steered his philanthropic adventures toward the respected Foundation for

Youth in his community of Columbus, Indiana. Local journalist Mark Webber calls Walter "one of Columbus' best known adventurers."

In May 2018, at age 70, Walter completed another international fund-raising expedition to scholarship youth who participated in FFY's wellness activities. "I've lived in Columbus since 1972, and after helping my hospitals in other towns I wanted to give back to my own community in the same way." As a certified grief counselor, his retirement activities also include co-facilitating three grief groups, including one for bereft parents.

How does one prepare to interview such a force of nature? Photographs show a strong looking man with a full head of gray hair and an enormous smile, especially when pointing to a mountain peak. He is a beloved family man as well as, "Poppa" to two sons and two grandchildren. He shares his activities with communities of friends saying "a lot of my life has been about friend making and friend keeping."

Walter has a disarming friendliness and candor. He's eager to be humble, but doesn't shy away from his spirituality or inspirational messages. When we spoke Walter had just returned from a 22 day adventure that included a 12 day hike across England to raise money for wellness programs for the young people of Columbus.

"Have you always been concerned with wellness?" I asked him.

"It started at an early age for me," he said. "Heart disease runs in my family and killed my father when I was only nine years old. My brother died at age 48. I wanted to live a long, full life."

Wally and his brother grew up in Bedford, Indiana, raised by strong, faithful women of Italian descent. Walter calls his mother "the Italiano queen of the kitchen" who worked as a telephone operator for 42 years. After their father died his aunt Angie, a compassionate and generous woman who never married, joined her sister to help raise her nephews. He describes her as a bold and fearless woman who modeled the attributes of courage, exercise, health, nutrition, and academics that guided both her nephews.

"There was no middle ground with Aunt Angie," Wally said. "And she led us by example. She was an overweight child who fought obesity and won throughout her life, at a time when people didn't think much about exercise. She was my role model and imprinted wellness in me.

"From the 1940's through the '80's, after working at a limestone mill office (for 47 years), she would either play golf, tennis, bowl, or swim. And she walked. We didn't have a car until I was in junior high. She walked—uphill—to church every morning. We all walked. When you grow up in that atmosphere you gain insight into exercise and possibility thinking."

Walter shared that his mother died of heart disease also—a broken heart after his brother died so young. He feels she surrendered to illness. Aunt Angie did her best to keep his mother active, but she developed Parkinson's and then Alzheimer's disease. "They were very different people. When Angie passed at 95, she had scheduled a full day of sports activities on her last birthday."

Like Angie, Walter does not surrender to illness. He hoped to climb all seven summits, but had to settle for five. In 2012 while training for both Denali and Antartica, the remaining two mountains, Walter suffered a fall on Mount Rainier with significant health implications. A medical workup revealed three aneurysms in three separate body systems. The most serious involved family genetics and required open heart surgery.

"It was hard for me to believe that eight months earlier I stood at 21,000 feet on a mountain in Argentina." After the open heart surgery, doctors told him his days of technical high altitude climbing were over. Did he give up? Of course not! In 2017 he suffered a fractured hip in a bicycle accident, letting himself fall to keep from hitting a person in his path. He fretted for months with the confinement. As the hip healed, he quickly returned to training.

Wally re-imagined his adventures from a wellness perspective: going long rather than high. He walked across Spain's 490 miles of El Camino, visited Machu Pichu in Peru, and recently walked across England.

"Since turning 70 in February 2018, I confess my days of sleeping in tents and technical climbs in all sorts of mountaineering gear on perilous high peaks in crazy weather are behind me. But you can see I have a high level of wellness—and with Aunt Angie's bold spirit as part of me, her fearlessness and possibility thinking help me re-imagine how to help kids—just as she helped me and many others."

All these accomplishments aside, what makes Walter a truly unique retiree? I believe it's his capacity to change, his determination to accept and learn from trials, and his resilience.

"I'm a much more patient person, both physically and emotionally, since the bike accident and rehabilitation," he said. "My fundamental wisdom involves intentionality—discovering purpose. I also believe in re-imagining, which helped me so much after the Rainier fall and open heart surgery. I didn't quit adventure wellness, but figured out new ways to sustain my charity, stay active, and have adventures. I'm always willing to try new things."

A current example is pickleball. Walter has been a tennis fanatic since childhood, but the game is harder at age 70. Enter pickleball—a gentler racquet and net sport with a big following in Columbus, and spreading like wildfire across the country. Walter has already registered for a tournament.

He wisely states, "With all that heart disease in my family I have to take care of myself. One of my sons wants me to investigate yoga, which can relieve joint pain and stiffness, improve flexibility and balance, and support core strength. I might give it a try."

Typically, he signed up for a 30 day intensive yoga course.

When I asked Wally about advice for others, he said, "I've used certain principles to guide my life:

With little risk, there is little reward.

We need to make fun of ourselves.

If I don't believe in myself, no one else will believe in me.

Are you living the life intended for you? Are you living up to your potential?

"I am blessed."

He added: "A question I often ask people is, 'What does calmness beget?' Few know the answer. 'Calmness begets calmness.' This important attribute supports inner peace and promotes accord between others."

Wally consciously listens to his inner voice whose promptings encouraged him to climb the Seven Summits and form a nonprofit organization to fight childhood obesity. He also listened carefully to his beloved Aunt Angie who encouraged him toward wellness. In addition, spirituality plays a large role in his life. Both of his books reflect his inner spiritual journey as he faced the challenges of training, altitude, and climbing.

Walter's final words were "Do we sell ourselves short so we can hide in our comfort zones, where we tend to settle for mediocrity?"

Walter has written two books that share his adventures and philosophy: *Mount Everest and Mount Kilimanjaro* and *Mount Elbrus and Mount Kosciuszko*. I have a feeling more books will be coming. I know Wally will continue setting an example for retirees as his sphere of influence widens and he continues pursuing his purpose in life (and Aunt Angie's).

Walter Glover on Expedition

NOTES

Walter Glovers' books:

Mount Everest and Mount Kilimanjaro: Seven Mountain Story, Book I. Walter Glover, MTS, NorLightsPress, 2016.

Mount Elbrus and Mount Kosciuszko: Seven Mountain Story, Book II. Walter Glover, MTS, NorLightsPress, 2017.

Don't Give In, Keep At It

Carol Basili

(Patricia)

> *"Courage doesn't always roar, sometimes it's the quiet*
> *voice at the end of the day whispering 'I will try again*
> *tomorrow.'"* Mary Anne Radmacher

Have you ever met someone you immediately wanted to know better—a person you're sure will offer you a glimpse of wisdom and sage advice? That's how I felt about Carol when we met in a Group Active exercise class at the gym. I couldn't stop watching this darling woman of about 4 foot 10 inches with a noticeably curved spine, as she moved to the dance music in class. I watched for her every week and tried to get a place next to her. She became my muse each week as I pushed myself in my cardio work out. If she could do it, so could I!

One week Carol didn't appear and our instructor Angela told us she'd broken her hip in a ballroom dancing accident. Until that moment I never knew she competed in ballroom dancing contests. Unfortunately, during warm up exercises Carol was bumped by another dancer who wasn't paying attention. I worried about Carol and asked Angela for weekly updates. I wondered if Carol would ever come back to class.

Yes! Five months later she appeared and resumed her workouts. She stayed on the ground without using the workout risers, but continued on. What an inspiration! When a new Mat Pilates class started, both Carol and I joined. I began asking Carol about her exercise routine and was astonished to learn she was 84 years young. Oh, my goodness! I told myself, "Carol is a healthy lifestyle inspiration for everyone, no matter how old we are." I learned even more about Carol when she agreed to an interview for this book.

Carol's parents met when her Italian immigrant father delivered bread to her mother's house in Beverly, Massachusetts. With her father's blessing, Carol's mother and father dated and soon married. They moved to Springfield, Massachusetts where Carol was born. After the hurricane of 1938, they moved up the hill to the Six Corners neighborhood of Springfield.

Carol said, "I always loved working. I started young by picking tobacco and then worked at a department store."

After high school, while working as a store clerk, she attended a dance band performance where she met her future husband, a member of the band. They married two years later and remained together for 40 years. Unfortunately this marriage ended in divorce because of his infidelity. Always tough, Carol decided she would never look like some "poor thing" getting divorced. Instead, she would buy a new dress for court and start going to the gym. That was 21 years ago, and she still exercises six times a week.

"I decided I wouldn't let the divorce destroy me. I would take care of myself by going to the gym and eating right. Going to the gym for 21 years has been for my mental and physical health."

While raising four children Carol had attended Weight Watcher's classes and lost 25 pounds. She was recruited by one of her teachers to teach a class, which she agreed to do if it was within walking distance and one day a week. She had a five year old at home and didn't own a car. And so began a 45-year career with Weight Watcher's. The extra income helped the family finances and by the time her children left the home Carol was teaching 13 classes a week. She taught into her late 70's and only stopped when she was abruptly told, "This will be your last day."

Carol said she and another dismissed older teacher filed complaints in court against Weight Watchers for age discrimination. The claim was denied; they refiled the complaint and it was denied again. At that point she decided it was futile to continue her claim against such a large enterprise, and instead continued with certain clients on her own, providing free advice.

At age 78, Carol felt the time had come to do something interesting during her forced retirement. A friend gave her free tickets to a dancing class at Fred Astaire studio, and thus began Carol's dancing career. She thought, "Dance will get me through no job, just as the gym got me through the divorce."

Carol said, "I was the third oldest person in my dance classes at the studio, but that didn't stop me. I plowed ahead and took on the challenge. In a few months I started dancing with a partner 33 years younger than me, and we won dance competition after dance competition."

Carol still loves dancing and combines it with exercising at the gym six days a week. Although she lives on a fixed income, she's a good money manager and budgets for her gym membership, dance lessons, a chiropractor once a month, a massage therapist one time a month, and a monthly Reiki healer.

"I don't take any medications, even with my advance scoliosis," Carol said. "I think this regime I'm on will continue keeping me healthy."

In addition to a healthy diet, exercise, and seven hours of sleep a day, Carol keeps a daily ritual of Mass at 7:30 every morning and thanks God for her good health and family. She also maintains an active social calendar. She goes to movies with friends on Tuesdays, has a lunch out with friends one time a month, goes to a TOPS (take off pounds sensibly) class once a month, teaches a weekly dietary class at a retirement home, and regularly sees her children. When I interviewed her at her home, I was surprised to see her dining room table with ten chairs around it. She said, "I keep it that way because the children and grandchildren often come over for pot luck dinners."

Although Carol has had struggles in her retirement, especially when she broke her hip three years ago, she will not give up. She had two hip operations within two years. The first hip repair with pins wasn't successful and she developed painful necrosis; so she opted for a total hip replacement a year after the first surgery. Now, with a rod in her hip, she continues on.

"It's a good thing we can get new parts nowadays, like repairing our cars," she said. Each operation called for a six to eight week recovery period. During those times she set daily goals for herself, walking a bit more day to day, going from a walker to a cane, and finally up the stairs to the gym. She adapted her floor exercise routine and no longer uses the riser, but discovered spinning classes which she loves.

Carol follows the advice in Dan Buettner's book *The Blue Zones* for healthy aging:

- daily rituals,
- a good diet,
- exercise,
- purpose,
- and socialization.

In addition to this list, Buettner identifies four things people can do to increase life expectancy: Create an environment that encourages physical activity; set up your kitchen in such a way that you're not overeating; cultivate a sense of purpose; and surround yourself with the right people.

When asked for advice on retirement and aging, Carol without hesitation said, Find something to keep your mind and body busy; don't give in. Keep at it—stay busy!

I see too many people who give up as they age. They sleep late and have nothing to do, so they don't stay sharp. I get up at five o'clock every morning when the alarm goes off. I don't want to stay in bed—I'll do that when I'm dead. I like to get up and go out. For relaxation I love DVDs and books from the library.

"I live simply and I'm grateful for my four children, five grandchildren and two great grandchildren. I enjoy my life and friendships and will continue to dance as long as I'm able. And I try to think good thoughts. Don't use up my energy being angry—it will only give you wrinkles."

As I suspected the moment I saw her at the gym, Carol is a model of wisdom and living well. She uses every single one of the wellness dimensions, and with this spirit I'm sure she'll continue living a long, healthy, and active life.

Carol Basili and Dance Partner

NOTES

The Rewards of Dancing as You Age

In an article titled "Rewards of Dancing as You Age," author Ellen Hoffman highlights the value of dancing in retirement and describes how she incorporated this new type of fun and fitness into her life at age 71. She says:

"Most of us probably know instinctively that dancing is good exercise, and exercise is a good thing. Surfing the Internet I can see there is, in fact, quite a bit of interest in dancing for seniors; and its benefits for both mental and physical health are touted by a well-credentialed group of experts. Dancing appears often in The National Institute of Aging's lists of activities that can help you stave off or combat osteoporosis, arthritis and even Alzheimer's."

Hoffman quotes Dr. William Hall, a professor of medicine and geriatrician at the University of Rochester School of Medicine and Dentistry, who says the ideal dance for the older crowd is the tango. "If I ran the universe," he says in a video posted on the university website, "I would tell every old person...to learn the tango. The tango has everything at once...music, romance, you are required to have agility, flexibility, strength, and you have to appreciate music. It's the perfect exercise."

References

Dan Buettner, *The Blue Zones: Lessons for Living Longer from the People Who've Lived Longest.* (National Geographic, Washington D.C., 2010).

Ellen Hoffman, *Rewards of Dancing as You Age: Dancing regularly can help revitalize your mind and your body.* (Retrieved from Next Avenue: http://www.nextavenue.org/rewards-of-dancing-as-you-age/).

I Think I Failed at Retirement

Marilyn

(Patricia)

> *"Nothing can give you joy. Joy is uncaused and arises from within as the joy of Being....It is your natural state, not something that you need to work hard for or struggle to attain." —Eckhart Tolle*

"I think I failed retirement," lamented forty year veteran of teaching, Marilyn. "I always thought I'd be ready for it, but I definitely was not ready, and I don't know how I could have been. I seem to be a person who had to work through it for several years. It felt like retiring was a sort of grieving, a loss of the self I'd been for so many years. And learning to accept change—I've never been good at that."

Marilyn grew up the oldest of four in a family where both parents were teachers. She always knew she wanted to teach elementary school and she started right out of college. When she was around forty, her husband Tom's job took them to Western Massachusetts.

"I began teaching at an elementary school with a well-loved physical education teacher. He happened to turn sixty in the month of March that year and happily retired in June. I always thought retiring at sixty sounded like a good plan. Of course, at that time, sixty seemed light years away."

Marilyn went through her forties and fifties watching other teachers retire. "Most of them couldn't wait to leave. They'd grown hardened, tired of teaching and the children. They no longer enjoyed their jobs. Some even had chalkboards with a countdown calendar for retirement. I knew I didn't want to retire that way. I wanted to retire while I still loved teaching and being with children."

When Marilyn turned sixty, to her surprise she didn't feel quite ready to leave teaching. "Though the new teachers were getting younger and younger, I still felt effective as a teacher."

At sixty-plus years, Marilyn looks and acts younger. She is petite and trim, exercises often, and has a friendly, engaging personality that warms everyone who meets her. It isn't hard to understand why she didn't feel ready to retire.

However, she said, "Unexpectedly, when I was 61, both my husband and I experienced life threatening illnesses at the same time in May and June. Though we knew about my husband's scheduled surgery, my illness was totally unexpected. It was a long and arduous process for both of us to regain our strength."

Marilyn didn't want to permanently leave teaching due to illness and never go back. So, "I thought I'd recuperated well over the summer. I mistakenly thought I was ready to jump back into the 'zero to sixty' rat race in September."

She "bulled through" the beginning of the year, but her stamina wasn't at its peak. Did I mention Marilyn is the type of teacher who gives 150 percent? For her, not having the stamina to do the job extremely well wasn't good enough. The thought of retirement entered her mind again, but a daughter announced her engagement and Marilyn was off to the races, planning a wedding. "I then purposely put thinking about retirement on the back burner during that year."

In September when she was 62, her son and his family moved far away for his military assignment. "We wanted to get to know our new grandson, but my teaching schedule wouldn't allow long trips except in summer. I began to think I needed to face the music. But, looking back on it now, I know I was frightened and sad at the thought of giving up my identity as a teacher."

As Marilyn began thinking seriously about retirement, she spoke to her husband and friends and sought professional life transition counseling. She made lists and lists of pros and cons. Always at the top of the Pro list were her health and her grandson. The Con list included loss of identity and purpose, plus a big question mark as to what she'd do with the extra time. "I thought I needed to have that answered before I could retire."

Marilyn kept postponing writing the official letter of retirement. "Intellectually, I knew I had to write the letter because my health and staying healthy were so important. And I wanted to leave while I still loved teaching and the kids."

But as Marilyn says, the hard part of not hating your job is that it's SO hard to leave it. "Emotionally, I found retirement very difficult." Twice Marilyn put her resignation letter in her mailbox, and both times she took it out. Finally, "I asked my husband to go with me to one of the large blue mailboxes near our home to put the letter in. That way I couldn't take it out again! I put the letter in on June first, and I think I cried at least once every day until the last day I left school, June 18, at age 63."

Marilyn's decision to retire was extremely difficult, though she had good reasons based on health concerns and her grandchildren. She loved teaching and worried about missing her identity as a teacher, the structure teaching gave her life, and the joy of teaching children and interacting with colleagues. But, the stress of teaching also took a toll on her body. As a 150 percent teacher, she was always the last to leave each night and she worked on schoolwork during evenings and on weekends. She had to retire to live!

Then came her next step, entering retirement. Marilyn's husband, Tom had taken a "golden handshake" early retirement about a year earlier. Ironically, as Marilyn left teaching Tom began a career teaching at a local college as an adjunct professor.

Like most teachers, Marilyn was a planner. But she hadn't planned much to do in retirement, other than take care of her health and see her grandchild. Therefore, her first year proved difficult. She kept asking herself, "What am I going to do?" She'd always been involved in church activities, and exercise, so those things were already in place. But in the past she stayed so busy running from one engagement to another, that now time seemed to stand still.

She feels perplexed when people ask her what she is "doing" now. "I always wonder, should I run down a list of things? Should I just say what trip is next? What if I said, not too much? I still feel a little like I'm apologizing for not doing my usual million things. Yet, I have a friend who has told me she feels too busy in retirement. I definitely don't want to feel like that."

Now four years out in retirement, Marilyn has more perspective on her adjustment.

The first year I spent trying to wrap my head around this new idea. At four years into it now, I hear of new retirees who have the same feelings as I did that first year. Retirement is truly a whole new way of thinking. I worked on going through my basement after 25 years of living in our house. I traveled to see my children and their families every chance I could, and I spent time with my mom. I went to a lot of lunches with other retired friends, but there are just so many lunches one can do before it gets a bit overdone.

During the second year I spent more time with my mom. She moved to this area several years earlier and lived on her own near our home. She was very independent and joined several senior center and church groups. But, unfortunately, she started having more physical problems. At that point I liked having time to go with her to doctor appointments and be with her. Little did I know, she would suddenly and unexpectedly pass away during that second year. I still miss her.

The third year, in addition to settling all my mom's affairs as the executrix, going through all her things, giving away or selling her furniture and belongings, and selling her condo, my daughter had a baby. When our second grandchild came along, I was grateful not to be working, so I could help my daughter as needed. I didn't have to worry about getting back home in a certain amount of time. I remember thinking, 'Okay, this flexibility to be with my family when I'm needed (making a contribution to help the world) makes retirement feel all right.' But it took me until year three to start truly mending my heart from the retirement ache.

"Year four of retirement has just begun, and I finally feel like I know what I am doing. I did have a bit of a setback recently where I considered taking a part-time job in a school. It seemed like the perfect fit and a comfortable setting. However, my family and primary care doctor were very much against this idea because of my health. I knew intellectually that I had to finally put this idea to rest. But again, emotionally, I felt the 'teacher' pull that was difficult to resist."

As she summarizes the past three years, Marilyn realizes this phase of her life has been a process of letting go; releasing her teacher identity, getting rid of accumulated memorabilia in her basement, and hardest of all, letting go of her mom. But through this letting go, she has been able to start to fully embrace retirement.

"Though it took more time than I ever imagined, I think I'm finally coming to terms with this huge change in my life. I'm trying to realize now that I still contribute to the world, but in a different way—through spending precious time with my husband of over forty years and my special grandchildren; through the various volunteer and church groups; through the blessings of new friendships, and while it may sound hokey, just appreciating each new day with gratitude and as a wonderful gift."

Marilyn has learned she is not a failure at retirement, just a slow-to-warm-up retiree who has now bloomed and learned to BE present in the moment!

The Part-Time Working Mom Retires

Jean Cantwell

(Patricia)

"Movement is a medicine for creating change in a person's physical, emotional, and mental states." —Carol Welch

When discussing retirement we often fail to consider women who don't work outside the home, or women who work part-time while raising their children. This group of moms is a significant part of our population in the United States and an important one to include in this book. How do women adjust to "early" retirement when they've been stay at home mothers? When and why do they decide to work part-time? How do they adjust to the empty nest?

I selected Jean as an example of a woman who chose to be a stay at home mom, then adjusted to working part-time, and finally re-adjusted to staying home to help with her grandchildren. Finally she transitioned to a life of her own in retirement. In spite of these adjustment challenges, Jean exemplifies healthy aging, especially in the physical and social realm.

I met Jean, age 78, at the local community center where she regularly swims. I watched daily as she greeted everyone with a friendly smile and frequent hugs. At six feet in height with short-cropped white hair, a lean body, and bright blue eyes, Jean lights up a room when she enters. She has an infectious laugh and exudes health. Jean's long neck is accentuated by the beautiful assortment of dangly earrings she wears.

Jean grew up the middle of three children; their father a banker and their mother a nurse. Jean describes her father as a quiet man who appreciated music. He played the piano and Jean says "At home I learned to love music. In those days we only had a radio and record player, but I attended the Springfield Symphony with my mother. I also learned from my parents to love gardening. My mother came from a farm in New Hampshire and she taught my father all about gardening. We had a large piece of property and grew grapes (we made jelly and grape juice), raspberries, rhubarb, and an apple orchard. My mother canned fruits and vegetables for winter."

Jean goes on to describe her mother as the disciplinarian. Even though I had a younger sister and older brother, I got most of the discipline. I didn't take studying and chores seriously and was often reprimanded. I began working in my teens babysitting and then worked in the kitchen of a local rest home. One summer I worked in the tobacco fields. After high school, I attended a local college for two years and studied secretarial science.

"I worked summer office jobs during college and after graduating I took a full time position as a secretary to the superintendent of schools. I was married at twenty-one and my husband David and I decided I'd stay home to raise our children and he would work outside the home. Six years into marriage I began working part-time to help with expenses. I worked three nights a week from three to eleven as a secretary at the local hospital. I stayed at that job for twenty years."

Jean's story is far from perfect: At thirty-three years of age she became a widow with three children under the age of eleven. Her husband of twelve years died of leukemia, which meant she needed to keep working to support her children. Jean related, After ten years of marriage David was diagnosed with leukemia. He'd been coming home from work and taking care of our kids at night when I worked part-time. This turned out to be a blessing because our kids knew their dad well before losing him. He was only thirty-five. Needless to say, our lives drastically changed. I became the sole parent caring for my children while working outside the home. It was a difficult time for me.

When David was diagnosed, I knew I had to stay well for my kids, so I started watching my health. I'd always been chubby, which was a big concern to my mother. She reprimanded me for eating the wrong foods. After my husband's death, I became much more careful about eating healthy and exercising.

Jean shared an article she wrote for the local newspaper in 1972: "I lost seventy pounds, but it took one and a half years to do it. No gimmicks, no pills. I just cut down. Instead of a helping of potatoes, for instance, I only took a bite or two. The only dietetic substitution I used was for sugar. If I felt I had to eat a certain food, I took ONLY A BITE. That worked well for me. I did try to eat balanced meals. A little exercise helps also. This is just one of many ways to diet, but I enjoyed it. Especially the results!"

Jean has kept this weight off for forty years with a healthy diet and regular exercise.

In the Spring following David's death, Jean hired a carpenter, Bruce, to finish an addition on her home that David and she had started. A year later, Bruce re-contacted her and they began dating. Three years later they married when the children were 16, 14, and 11 years of age. Bruce and Jean just celebrated their 40th wedding anniversary.

Jean decided to keep working part-time after Bruce and she married.

"What about your retirement?" I asked.

Jean said, "My daughter had a baby when she was in high school. She wanted to finish high school so it was easier for me to leave work and take care of my grandchild. Bruce and I decided we could afford to have me at home; we knew we could cut our spending and still take care of needed expenses."

So, Jean's first retirement began with caring for her grandson. Although she loved helping her daughter, she wrote about the down side in a 1982 newspaper article titled, Grandparents Playing Parents: "Our main concern has been taking care of our grandson. I'm sure many grandparents are thrilled to be needed, but I was so looking forward to the empty nest syndrome. Now, when I should be loving and cuddling my grandson, I end up scolding and correcting him."

True retirement only came for Jean within the last ten years when her final grandchild went off to school.

Jean loves retirement. She says, "The only thing that surprised me in retirement is how fast time goes by and how busy I am. I garden, work outdoors, and swim five days a week. I became a lifeguard in my forties so I could teach the Swimnastics class. I also was part of a synchronized swimming group, all of us in our forties and fifties. We were very good and laughed a lot. At home I do simple exercises to keep my joints moving, and in my sixties I started a class to improve balance and strength. I just started a mindfulness yoga class, which I absolutely love."

Jean does miss the socialization of work. "I loved meeting and dealing with new people at the hospital. I learned so much. But now I love meeting the people I swim with. We get together once or twice a year at my house for pot luck brunches. Once in a while I have a theme of sorts for the brunch, such as a tea party, ice cream social, a pajama party, or a Halloween party. We are elders having a great time and age from our 60's through 90's."

Jean goes on, "I've never had a problem with aging. I feel my life eased up as I got older. I feel more relaxed. I became a little less structured and began enjoying my time a lot more than when I was on a strict schedule of parenting and part-time work."

Jean decided in her sixties to volunteer with an Ombudsman program for the Commonwealth of Massachusetts. That experience reinforced her responsibility for taking care of herself the best she could. "I learned so much by listening to elders who've been there, done that."

"What advice do you have for future retirees," I asked.

"Take care of your health now, so when retirement comes you'll be able to enjoy the time you earned. It's now your time!"

Jean wanted to end with a quote she recently read in Reader's Digest magazine: "Take care of your body as though you're going to need it for 100 years, because you might!"

Thank you, Jean for sharing your story with its ups and downs, and for your will to get healthy and live a fulfilling life into your seventies and eighties....and perhaps nineties....or 100's.

NOTES

In a review in the *Journal of Applied Physiology* that explored the importance of exercise, the authors stated: "Make no mistake, our society, and even the world's population in general, is truly at war against a common enemy. That enemy is modern chronic disease."

In a later review, Dr. Frank Booth states we're facing a silent enemy: the sedentary lifestyle. His solution: "Every US adult should accumulate 30 minutes or more of moderate-intensity physical activity on most, and preferably all, days of the week. Adults who engage in moderate-intensity physical activity – i.e., enough to expend 200 calories per day—can expect many health benefits."

References

Frank Booth and Manu Chakravarthy. "Cost and Consequences of Sedentary Living: New Battleground For an Old Enemy." (President's council on Physical fitness and Sports, *Research Digest*, series 3, no. 16, March, 2002) 774-787.

Basic Health Guidelines for Older Adults
(Helene)

As we grow older, eating well, exercising, and taking care of our bodies becomes more important every year. Numerous studies show that a healthy diet and physical activity make a dramatic difference in quality of life for senior citizens—and we're never too old to enjoy these benefits. Even modest lifestyle changes can lead to an immediate difference in energy levels and enjoyment of life. This is an overview of the most important ingredients for healthy aging.

Basic Medical Care

Don't neglect your annual physical examination. This appointment gives you an excellent chance to ask health concern questions, have your medications refilled, review blood work results (some PCP's like to order annual blood tests), and receive vaccinations. Don't hesitate to mention problems you've been having even if they seem minor to you, including medication side effects and mental changes.

As we age, our immune systems become less robust, placing us at risk for diseases with serious and possibly life-threatening complications. Vaccinations can prevent some of these issues. Four vaccines are recommended for older adults:

1. Annual Flu Vaccine, preferably the high dose variety designed for more effectiveness for patients over 65.

2. Shingles vaccine which has a newer version that is touted to be 90% effective for up to four years.

3. Tdap vaccine for tetanus, diphtheria, and pertussis (whooping cough which is making an unfortunate comeback and is very dangerous for children under 12 months of age). A booster shot for tetanus and diphtheria is due every ten years. This

vaccine is especially important for grandparents who have contact with young grandchildren.

4. pneumonia vaccine (both kinds one year apart).

Your annual physical is the perfect time for the PCP to order recommended diagnostic tests that may be due, including:

- Annual mammography to rule out breast cancer.
- Periodic bone densitometry to monitor any development of osteoporosis (bone thinning).
- Periodic colonoscopy beginning at age 50 and every 3 to10 years thereafter, depending on results of the test and family or personal history.
- Dental Cleanings and Exams: Dental and gum disease may contribute to the decline of general medical health and also may be symptomatic of more systemic illness. Therefore, it's important to take care of your teeth.
- Eye Exams are essential to monitor for glaucoma, macular degeneration, and cataracts. All these medical conditions are treatable, if not treated can greatly impair your vision. Impaired vision is a contributor to the falls of older people.
- Hearing tests by a qualified audiologist: These tests will rule out significant hearing loss that can affect the quality of life, jeopardize your safety, and contribute to social isolation.

Consider Your Diet

As adults grow older we need fewer total calories, but higher amounts of some nutrients.

Growing older is no excuse to stop watching what we eat. A healthy diet will help you live longer, feel better, and enjoy an active lifestyle. Diet may also improve—or at least help preserve— our mental abilities. Rush University Medical Center developed a diet to promote brain health (aptly called MIND) that is a hybrid of the Mediterranean diet and the DASH diet that fights hypertension. Learn more about the MIND diet for beginners at: www.healthline.com/nutrition/mind-diet

"Foods that promote brain health, including vegetables, berries, fish and olive oil, are included in the MIND diet" said Dr. Laurel J. Cherian, a vascular neurologist and assistant professor in Rush's Department of Neurological Sciences. The best diet includes a healthy amount of food from all food groups, but avoids high fat, red meats, processed and fatty fried foods, and excess sugar or sugary drinks. Cutting down on the size of food portions has also been linked to longevity.

To make sure all your nutritional needs are met, consider taking supplements such as a multivitamin for seniors. The vitamin B's and antioxidants protect against cell damage that occurs in aging. Growing older may also lead to bone loss. Calcium, vitamin D, and magnesium supplements help maintain bone density. Weight bearing exercise also strengthens bones. People who exercise actually have healthier cells than those who do not.

Loss of muscle mass, known as sarcopenia, also tends to occur with aging. Less muscle can lead to more fat, which produces inflammatory compounds that fuel deadly chronic diseases, such as heart disease and cancer. Weakened muscles contribute to falls that can be so dangerous as we age. Fish oil supplements help protect against chronic inflammation and is protective for the muscles, heart and brain. Adequate protein in your diet will help prevent muscle breakdown and build new muscles.

The Benefits of Exercise

Experts suggest adults should try to get 2.5 hours of aerobic exercise every week and do strength training twice a week. Weight bearing exercise strengthens bones. Along with improving overall health and helping you feel better, exercise is also an important way to guard against falls and improve your balance. If these goals seem unrealistic, remember that ANY exercise is better than none, including short walks of ten minutes several times a day. Take the stairs instead of an elevator if you can manage it. Park your car a distance from your destination and walk there.

Sitting for hours at a desk or in front of the TV is now identified as a health crisis, perhaps as significant as smoking. As one publication stated, "Sitting is the new smoking." Being overweight is only part of the story, because we can be overweight and fit, or thin and unfit. No matter what your body shape, being sedentary does not equate with being healthy. Experts say that breaking up sitting with even light activity, such as walking around the room, can have a positive impact on your health.

For 25 years seniors with Medicare have been eligible to join Silver Sneakers, a free fitness program available in gym and fitness centers in the network. This excellent program provides classes, socialization, and activities run by certified instructors. Consider joining today: www.silversneakers.com.

Consider practicing yoga. Yoga strengthens the body, works against bone loss, improves balance and safety, and quiets the mind (something we can all benefit from!)

Are You Sleep Deprived?

Get seven hours of sleep, the amount associated with longevity. John Whyte, M.D. notes that people tend to sleep less soundly and for fewer hours after age 50. Severe sleep problems shouldn't be ignored because they will increase risk for heart disease, diabetes, and other serious conditions.

Sleeping pills offer a quick fix, especially in TV commercials, but these meds tend to stop working after a while, can lead to dependence, grogginess the next day, and increased risk for falls.

Nighttime falls are all too common with older folks, for several reasons. We tend to have nighttime urinary frequency that has us walking in the dark while half asleep. Throw rugs and items on the floor can lead to falling. Various medications (SSRI antidepressants in particular) and alcohol before bedtime can alter sleep patterns and create problems with balance. Confusion during the night can be a symptom of early-stage dementia, and needs to be reported to the PCP.

Snoring affects the sleep of everyone. Severe and frequent snoring may be caused by breathing issues, such as obstructive sleep apnea. Beyond the irritation of snoring, this common condition poses health risks for heart attacks, high blood pressure, type 2 diabetes, stroke, and depression. If you suspect sleep apnea, don't ignore the symptoms. Your PCP can order a sleep study. A breathing machine called CPAP (continuous positive airway pressure) can remedy the problem and give you quieter, more restful, and safer sleep.

Don't Overdo Alcohol

Our bodies handle alcohol differently as we age. You may keep the same drinking habits, but your body has changed and is more sensitive to negative effects of alcohol. Alcoholism often develops in later years of life, and more and more retirement communities are being identified as places for "partying." These may be the same communities that contribute to an uptick in sexually transmitted disease among seniors.

Although the benefits of red wine to health have been documented, over-use of alcohol can contribute to falls and driving impaired. Drinking alcohol doesn't go well with many prescription meds, and with some medications any amount of alcohol may cause serious health issues.

Know Your Medications

Be sure to learn about medications prescribed for you, including what each drug is supposed to do, potential side effects, and possible interactions with your other medications or food. Too many people depend on their healthcare providers to know these things for them. You are responsible for your own health. Be proactive!

Many older people are prescribed opioids to help painful conditions associated with aging, such as arthritis. Unfortunately, senior citizens have become dependent on these medications and have contributed to our country's opioid crisis. Cash strapped seniors have sold their prescriptions; others have their medications stolen by relatives, friends, and caregivers and sold to addicts. Use caution with any potentially sedating or addictive medication which can suppress respirations and lead to sudden death. Take these medications as prescribed and only as long as necessary. Dispose of them in a safe container found in some pharmacies.

Don't Smoke!

If you do smoke, consider talking with your PCP about methods to help you kick the habit. Sadly, the longer you smoke the more likely you will develop cancer or COPD (chronic obstructive pulmonary disease) and be dependent on portable oxygen tanks to survive. An excellent resource for smokers trying to quit is: *www.cdc.gov/tobacco/campaign/tips/*.

References

Hallie Levine. "The 4 Vaccines Older Adults Need: Why You Should Get Them and How Well They Work," (*Consumer Reports.org*, October 20, 2017). https://www.consumerreports.org/vaccines/vaccines-older-adults-need/

Michael Grossman., *The Vitality Connection: Ten Practical Ways to Optimize Your Health and Reverse the Aging Process.* (Vitality Press Publications, 2003).

Picard, Andre, "Why the Sedentary Life is Killing Us," The Globe and Mail, Inc. October 15, 2013; updated May 9, 2018. https://www.theglobeandmail.com/life/health-and-fitness/health/why-the-sedentary-life-is-killing-us/article4613704/

Our Stories

I Just Can't Stop: Helene's Retirement Story

The first time I considered my own retirement was in 1968, shortly after Whiting and I married. We both received a social security document that listed 2010 as our retirement year. We doubled over in laughter at a year so far in the future and a date right out of Star Trek—2010. Seriously?

My father retired in 1972 at age 62—my first exposure to retirement. That initiated a time of three large moves and episodic world travel. Most significantly, he and my mother moved from their native NJ to Massachusetts to be six blocks from me, my husband and two small daughters. That move had a huge influence on us as you will later see.

In 2015, following 47 years of working as a psychiatric nurse, my retirement was celebrated at age 70. That sounds like a nice round retirement age, right? Wrong! My first book with coauthor Patricia Peters Martin, Ph.D. (*The Other Couch: Discovering Women's*

Wisdom in Therapy) would soon be published and I was heading off on a two month vacation. But before I left, even before the lovely retirement party, I sidled up to the agency VP and said, "I've been thinking, there are a handful of patients I'm really having a hard time giving up. Do you think it would be possible for me to work, say, two days a month?"

Truth be told, I was also having trouble giving up the work relationships with the young women my daughters' age who've helped me feel young. Writing a book honoring our inspiring patients underscored how much those relationship mean to me. Patricia and I have an important commonality: We love our patients and love sharing their empowering and inspiring stories.

Fast forward to 2018. Most weeks I work one day and occasionally more when the agency needs coverage. But life has shifted again. In our previous book I discussed how my husband and I had adjusted to being grandchildless (our daughters' choices) and the huge paradigm shift when they changed their minds.

Our only grandchild Henry is now five. His mother Katharine and his father now live in New Jersey. She has fond memories of my parents living near our home in Massachusetts. When I began working full time at the medical center, the girls would spend one day a week with them. They were available for the occasional emergency pick up or on sick days. Katharine works in Manhattan and worries about Henry when she isn't readily available. She has already developed a close network of friends who help each other out, but she wanted more.

Last year our cunning Katharine innocently said, "I was thinking (that phrase prefaces many seismic changes in our family) wouldn't it be easier for you and Dad to sell the co-op in Brooklyn (which we had enjoyed for 24 years) and rent an apartment near us so you can visit and stay longer?"

Ka-Boom! You make a suggestion to a Houston woman and it is a done deal. Four months after the idea's inception we were moving across the East River. Now we pick up Henry early from pre-school when we're in town, work on his swimming skills, and read with him. Grandpa Duff and Meme couldn't be happier about sharing more of his life.

I need to discuss my amazing husband who retired from his 40 year banking career at age 62 in 2007. That timing allowed him to be available to my ailing father who passed away that year at 95 (can you imagine 33 years of retirement?) and his mother who also had severe medical problems and passed in 2008. He was instrumental in helping all our parents transition to beautiful retirement communities nearby. Our parents' positive experiences in their retirement communities will pave the way for Whiting and me to make a transition to such a community in the near future.

Besides being a patient, loving caregiver, Whiting was able to explore the Adventurer in him, based on the retirement path identified by Nancy Schlossberg. He had an opportunity to work on his skiing while enjoying old friends. He nourished his love of theater by joining the board of directors of a theater company in the Berkshires. This association expanded our friendships as well. And, most unexpectedly, Whiting turned out to be an excellent chef. He showed little interest in cooking early in our marriage, but during my brief immobility from foot surgery a cooking class inspired what turned into a healthy, enjoyable, and much appreciated hobby. He focuses on healthy foods, luckily for both of us. Whiting gets into the zone with cooking and turns boring tasks into meditation in motion. Now we both enjoy cooking shows. My job is to discover new recipes for him. Whiting also uses his culinary and nurturing skills to bring the family together. There is something special about sharing a meal cooked by a loving chef.

One secret to our happy retirement is having personal space to pursue individual interests and grow. We respect and admire one another's success. While we enjoy time together, time with friends and family, traveling, and going to the theater, each of us makes time for our special interests. My most productive writing times happen when Whiting goes off skiing or hiking, being an Adventurer.

While my career as an advanced practice psychiatric nurse is winding down, I'm not quite ready to stop. Instead of being an Adventurer, I am more like one of Schlossberg's Continuers. I'm beginning to picture another transition that will include more "Henry time." The twists and turns of our lives have enhanced our social connections with unexpected and inspiring people. Now we're meeting friends of our daughters and, as our world continues to expand, we realize how lucky we are.

In this book, Patricia and I have stressed the importance of meaning and purpose in life as we age. My husband and I have a shared purpose: enjoying and supporting our family and each other. I realize my purpose throughout my career has been listening to and honoring the stories I've had the privilege of hearing. In this book we honor the unique journeys of special people who are writing the "next chapters" of their lives.

Helene and Whiting Houston
at the theatre

Whiting Houston cooking
with Henry

References

Nancy Schlossberg, Ed.D. *Too Young to Be Old: Love, Learn, Work, and Play as You Age* (APA LifeTools; 1 edition, 2017).

On The Cusp: Patricia Ponders Her Next Move

Do you ever look in the mirror and ask yourself, "Who is this person?"

Actually, I rarely look in the mirror these days, unless I'm searching for unwanted hair on my chin to pluck. Ugh! Such is the lot of losing estrogen as we hit that post-menopausal age. Yet, I have to admit I don't miss my menstrual cycle one bit. I do wonder often where the years went and, even though I still feel inside like the twenty and thirty year old of the past (well, maybe 40 or 50 year old), when I look at my reflection, I recognize the changes in my face and body. Gravity is a powerful force!

I have to admit, I can still do a reasonable headstand after years and years of yoga, which I discovered in 1972 as a freshman in college. Yoga wasn't in vogue back then. In fact, very few in the Western world had even heard of it. This practice has been a salvation throughout my life. Focus, core strength, and balance.... all thanks to my yoga practice.

As a consolation prize for aging, I am also wiser and have connected with my intuitive side. As the years pass, I wonder what lies ahead in the future. My husband and I talk now and again about retirement. We are both good savers, so we feel comfortable about our financial future. But, ask me again in June, after we've paid for two daughters' weddings within eight months. Yikes!

The truth is, I can't imagine being retired yet. At 63, I still feel young and have energy for my psychology practice. As long as my brain holds out, I can still do the work of helping others in psychotherapy. I shortened my work week over the past five years, going down to four days a week, and now I'm practicing three days a week. I'm fortunate to have this kind of flexibility in my profession as a private practice clinical psychologist. If I had to work five days every week, I might not be so reluctant to retire.

As I think about why I'm not ready to retire, I settle on a few reasons: purpose, identity, finances, and involvement.

When you truly love what you're doing in life, it doesn't feel like drudgery. I promised myself that when I get bored or feel I can no longer be effective, I will close up shop. That is not a reality now, but the day will come within a decade or two. As I say that, I reflect on my maternal grandmother who ran a beauty shop in Atlantic City until she was 82 years old, and my father who died at 90 while still president of a small insurance company. So maybe it's in the genes. We are long livers, and long workers in my family.

My active husband, Jim, who is 65, talks vaguely about retirement in the years ahead. He is a busy, full time attorney in our town of Springfield, Massachusetts. Jim is probably one of the busiest people I've ever known, both in his professional life, volunteer activities, and commitment to family. He's also one of the best fathers I know. Lucky me; I guessed he'd be a great dad, and my youthful prophesy proved true.

When Jim retires, I'm sure he'll continue with his daily three mile runs, playing sports with friends, and his commitments to volunteering and family. He's up early every morning and the first to get on skype to see our grandchildren in DC. I have to sometimes remind him it's hard on our daughter to have us enter their busy morning routine every day. He reluctantly agrees, and chomps at the bit until the time is right to make the call. How he loves them all!

I'm fortunate to have parents who were active and alert into their 90's. My Dad told me his secret to aging: "Always have something to look forward to, always be actively learning something new, and stay physically active." He was learning Italian in his 80's when we planned a trip to Italy. He'd begin planning his next trip as soon as he returned home from one voyage. He made model boats for his entire family (wife, brother, 5 children and 14 grandchildren) until the day he died. Dad was amazing, and a great role model.

And then there's my mom, with whom I live three months a year when she stays with us in New Hampshire. She and Dad joined my family every summer starting in 1993, after they had sold their lake cottage in southern Indiana. Each summer they came to be with my clan and escape the heat of Mobile, Alabama where they settled near my sister. They came every summer except 2013, which was the last summer of my father's life as he faced the terminal diagnosis of pulmonary fibrosis. But, God bless him, he still talked about coming even into July, two months before he died.

One remarkable thing about Mom is that she decided to keep coming to New Hampshire, even without Dad. She'd never flown on an airplane by herself, but ventured out in 2014 at the age of 87 and flew to Manchester, NH, via Charlotte, N.C. She has come here every summer since. We spend wonderful time together, sitting on the deck or screened porch, reminiscing about the past, and looking forward to weddings and births in the present and future. She terribly misses my dad, but is determined she will live on until her Creator lets her know it's her time.

She is my role model for aging. Mom has a selfless way about her and, as she looks toward her final days, she decided her purpose now, to the best of her ability, is to pass on to her children and grandchildren the wisdom of life she has attained. She watches the Mass on TV every morning, and asks the Holy Spirit to help her find the right words to reach her children and grandchildren. I marvel at this generous spirit!

As I venture into my retirement years, I will carry the role model of two awesome parents—both wise in unique ways: Dad's intellectual/occupational prowess and my mom's emotional/spiritual intelligence.

I will continue with yoga, writing, and exploring my creativity, while also making time for family and friends. I started the game of golf and find that intermittent random reinforcement of a good shot keeps me coming back to this challenging game.

I hope my husband and I will enjoy the fruits of our labors, both financially and socially. Together, we will face the years ahead. And, God willing, we'll live to be elders who have something to share with the coming generations—along with time to travel—as we reach for the integrity and wisdom of old age.

Patsy, Jim, and Grandkids

Conclusion

Standing on Her Shoulders

Venessa O'Brien

(Helene)

> *"Inside we are ageless...and when we talk to ourselves, it's the same age of the person we were talking to when we were little. It's the body that is changing around that ageless center."* —*David Lynch*

In 2013, Venessa O'Brien, age 94, received the Standing on Her Shoulders award from the Women's Fund of Western Massachusetts. This award celebrated outstanding risk-takers and innovators who through their determination and leadership have increased opportunities and blazed trails. The Women's Fund chose to honor elder women whose stories have not been told or are not known beyond their immediate circles. Venessa was nominated by Bay Path College, now known as Bay Path University.

Venessa came from a small town in Maine (pop. 1000). She originally planned to attend the University of Maine like her older brother, but decided to move to Springfield, Massachusetts, a then bustling city of 150,000, to attend the Bay Path Institute, a business school. After 48 weeks of intensive study, she graduated in 1938.

Venessa's many gifts include working hard, problem solving, and making lifelong friends everywhere she goes. Upon arriving in Springfield she befriended a family who provided her a home as she studied and remain her second family to this day. She later stayed at the YWCA as many young women did in those years.

After graduation Venessa immediately accepted a job with the Springfield office of General Electric. She quickly realized the men she worked with were doing a lot more interesting things than filing. Soon she began covering the lunch hour alone and would field complex technical questions from clients. She devoured books in the office and the sales engineers she covered for encouraged her initiative. According to the government, a sales engineer "sells complex scientific and technological products or services to businesses. They must have extensive knowledge of the products' parts and functions and must understand the scientific processes that make these products work." This was exactly the work Venessa did for many years, but without the engineering degree, salary, or job title.

When a position for a sales engineer opened, her male supervisor told her over a three hour lunch that he couldn't give her the job because it entailed travel and "a lot of wolves are out there." With a little prodding from me, Venessa admits she felt angry about being denied the job.

About 1970, General Electric was closing Venessa's Springfield office and the two remaining sales engineers retired. She finally received the position of sales engineer in a Connecticut office, the first female in the entire company hired for that position. She continued for 12 years, successfully working with important and lucrative accounts.

She told me, "I won so many wonderful incentive trips the company changed the sales requirements to make winning awards more difficult. I also traveled for my work and loved it." She looked forward to her 1982 retirement with many plans for traveling with the friends she easily met during her adventures.

Venessa believes she inherited strength from her family. Her father was a merchant marine, gone much of the time. Her mother learned to be independent as she raised her three children. She learned to drive and bought a car much earlier than most women in the 1920s and 1930s. She worked in an office as well. Venessa's father was drafted and in World War II helped ferry soldiers over the English Channel as a lieutenant colonel. She said, "He didn't like speaking of the ship hitting mines, but I know he never lost a man."

Despite her beauty, positive nature, and fun-loving spirit, Venessa never married. "I didn't have time" she said with a coy smile. She lives in a lovely ranch home decorated with the color blue and scores of butterflies collected over the years.

She said, "As soon as people realized the name Venessa means butterfly they started giving me butterflies. I love it."

Her home reflects her creative side and the night classes she took in drapery making, upholstery, and wood-working. She enjoyed interior decoration for herself and lucky friends. She is a sharp dresser who took classes in millinery and tailoring as well.

As we sat enjoying the lunch she prepared at a table in the dining room overlooking a winter backyard, I couldn't help but be amazed that this vibrant woman would soon celebrate her 99th birthday. She knew I was interviewing her because I felt she was a wonderful example of healthy aging.

"How do you handle retirement, and to what do you attribute your long life?" I asked.

"I stay busy," she said. And indeed she does. She has traveled the world. Her last trip was to China in 2012 accompanying Bay Path Students. She loves to talk about going on the Great Wall twice.

She stays close to some of the students because of an endowed scholarship she created. The grateful students write to her, one encouraging her to visit in Africa. One of Venessa's favorite trips was South Africa. A woman and daughter she met on another trip invited her to go on a Fordham sponsored tour that was unforgettable.

"I am a people person" Venessa said, and indeed she is. When she isn't traveling she volunteers at her church (where she is famous for her deviled eggs) and is at the Longmeadow Adult and Senior Center where she manages the Maple Tree Gift Shop and has volunteered for 20 years.

Throughout her life Venessa has befriended younger people. Her niece and grandnieces cherish their relationship with her and even asked her to be the maid of honor at their weddings, despite a 60 year age difference. I suspect her relationships and ease with younger people contribute to the "girlishness" that emanates from her animated and always smiling face.

Earlier in her retirement, Venessa stayed physically active, continuing to ski ("I skied downhill all over the world; my retirement gift was cross country skis.") She also played golf. Now she participates in exercise classes at the Senior Center.

She said, "After retirement I also spent several years working with my niece's husband on various entrepreneurial ventures, doing the books, working in his bookstores, working as a travel consultant." She remained close with her niece and her family who now live in Myrtle Beach and would love for her to join them. Her niece calls almost every day to check in. Venessa is dearly loved. However, Venessa's heart is where her friends are, and she isn't inclined to move. She smiled as she looked around her home and said, "I guess it will be my family's job to clean it out someday."

As we discussed the strongest predictors of a long life, she agreed that social interaction is vital. "I also try to exercise two times a week. I keep busy doing things I like to do, and I try to eat properly and follow a good diet. I also try to keep a positive attitude."

She admitted she's lucky to not suffer from any "infirmities." As we discussed the importance of social interaction, I shared the thoughts of Ralph Warner in his book *Get a Life: You Don't Need a Million to Retire Well*. In his chapter "Friends" he speaks of the importance of finding friends from all aspects of your life; welcoming younger friends who will survive you and older friends who have wisdom to share. I'm hoping Venessa and I are a good match!

Venessa, the Year of Her Promotion at GE   *Venessa O'Brien*

References

Ralph Warner, *Get a Life: You Don't Need a Million to Retire Well*. NOLO, 2004.

Well-Come to Healthy Aging

(Helene)

By now it must be clear that all eight dimensions of wellness are important to a satisfying third act of our lives. Neglecting any one of them can diminish the pleasure of retirement, while exploring new possibilities may actually lengthen our lives.

What stood out as you read about Venessa's 99 years? Good genetics helped with longevity, but she supplemented this with occupational and intellectual achievements and an active lifestyle that protected her health. Venessa also enjoys a strong spiritual life: She joined a church in 1937 and dove headlong into participating. She stimulated her creativity by learning about interior decoration and now enjoys managing a gift shop that helps support a community adult center. Venessa's many years of work with a giant corporation ensured her financial health.

Research—and common sense—associate poor physical health, lack of exercise, and obesity with early death. Recent studies reveal that of all the predictors of longevity we know, the greatest predictors of a long life are social integration (frequent daily interactions with many people) and close relationships (availability of people we can count on).

Using Venessa as an example, her relationships have never been shallow or self-serving. To this day she remains friends with many people she met as a young woman. Her roommate in her early Springfield career days is now in her 90's, married, and lives across the street from Venessa's suburban home. Friends she made on her many trips became traveling companions. Her brother's children and grandchildren treat her as they would a parent, with the concern and generosity we all wish for. She is a cherished friend to many.

We can all learn from Venessa, and it's just a question of opening our hearts. In her recently published book *Too Young to be Old*, expert and researcher Nancy K. Schlossberg, Ed.D. speaks to the importance of Positive Aging. She says, "I wanted to challenge ageism and help us all come to terms with our love-hate relationship with aging. But most importantly I wanted to suggest ways to face aging with creativity as people see the possibilities." Venessa is a perfect example of this way of life.

In his book *How We Age: A Doctor's Journey into the Heart of Growing Old*, Marc Agronin, M.D. identified ten tips for aging well, which he generously allowed us to share:

Ten Tips for Aging Well
1. Exercise Your Body
2. Exercise Your Brain
3. Fruits, Veggies, Fish
4. Relationships Count Most
5. Memory is More than Words
6. Know What Hurts
7. Be Wise
8. Count Your Blessings
9. Be Creative
10. Don't Worry, Be Happy

As you'll read in the poem that follows, "It takes meticulous attention to live in your 90's. The orchestration of wise doctors and attention and love from friends and family makes it a lively adventure, with plenty of thanks to God for the privilege."

References

Nancy K. Schlossberg, Ed.D., *Too Young to be Old* . (APA LifeTools; 1 edition (April 17, 2017).

Marc Agronin, M.D., *How We Age: A Doctor's Journey into the Heart of Growing Old*. (Da Capo Lifelong Books, 2011).

Downsizing Dilemma: What Do I Keep?
(Helene)

When thinking about retirement many people decide to downsize their lives. This might include evaluating priorities, moving to a smaller home, or just reducing the amount of accumulated stuff.

Deciding what stays with you when you downsize is probably the most time consuming and gut wrenching of all the steps. Taking a general inventory of possessions is a good way to start the process. The inventory will probably reveal many duplicate items: Does a person really need 30 pairs of shoes, four sets of socket wrenches, or an attic filled with memorabilia? Duplicates are the easiest things to cross off your list, so start with them.

Consider setting up a work area for sorting and evaluating items. Expert household organizers and those treating folks who hoard advise a three-pronged approach to sorting: things you keep, things you give away (to family, friends or charity), and items you'll throw away. A fourth consideration is what you might sell and to whom. This rational sorting process leads to quick progress that helps you feel less emotional. If you do feel overwhelmed, try setting a timer for 30 minutes and begin a single task, such as sorting shoes, clearing a cluttered shelf in the garage, or going through a bookcase.

The six month test is helpful for sorting. Ask yourself, "Have I used this item during the past six months? If not, then why do I need it?" Be suspicious of any answer that begins with, "I'll keep it just in case . . ."

Those of us who collect things or grew up with collectors see value in items most people would discard. I've held on to certain things for over 60 years because I feel someone will appreciate their value and enjoy them. If you're downsizing, this may be the time to set these items free to find new owners, such as family members who would enjoy your heirlooms.

During my downsizing process, Marie Kondo's book *The Life-Changing Magic of Tidying Up* helped me identify what's important enough to keep. She advises holding each object for a few moments to see if it "sparks joy." If it does, then you have a keeper!

Kondo advises readers to consider four factors that add value to our possessions: physical value, function, information, and emotional attachment. By far, emotional attachment is the greatest challenge because we tend to link inanimate objects with special memories. That's why, according to Kondo, beginning your sorting project with mementos spells certain failure. Save these special items for last, and when you reach that point make a ceremony of it. On page 116, Kondo says: "By handling each sentimental item and deciding what to discard, you process your past."

Other downsizing consultants suggest taking photos of treasured objects before you part with them. For me, a photo would bring little comfort compared to my three dimensional keepsakes but it certainly is a space saving option.

My husband Whiting and I just celebrated our 50th wedding anniversary. To mark this occasion and prepare for an eventual move to a retirement community we've been sorting through photos, letters, and archives of our current family and previous generations. In essence we are conducting a life review coinciding with a special date. For us, this process has been renewing and rewarding. We divided these files among family members and they've been welcomed and appreciated, adding to our shared reminiscing and family history.

I wish you the best of luck and success with your own downsizing journey.

Reference:

Marie Kondo: *The Life-Changing Magic of Tidying Up*, Ten Speed Press; 1st edition (October 14, 2014).

Poems by Fernande Gardner Alexander (1900-1990)

Fernande Alexander was an American writer and photographer who studied acting and performed in and directed theatrical productions. She wrote and published one act plays for women. The poems that follow were written in her own hand during the last decade of her life. They are shared with the permission of her daughter, Gay Wesson, who loves and misses her.

PRESCRIPTION:

15 Vitamins And 5 sure Drugs
Yo Ho Ho And a bottle of Scotch!
(2-3 oz. daily)
It Takes Meticulous Attention
To Live in your 90's.
The Orchestration of wise Doctors
And Attention, with Love,
From Friends and Family
Makes it a Lively Adventure,
with plenty of Thanks to God
For The Privilege.
Or Perhaps we'd Live
Our sure-footed Lives
Without Any Prescriptions?
Just Living As we've Always Lived,
Enjoying every Moment,
With God's Blessing?
Who Knows?

Fernande Alexander

January Ahhh! January — "My" Month!
Mother always said,
"No _nice_ girl tells her age.
Besides, it's No One's business."
     So I never tell.
But, now I am an Octogenarian,
I've become slightly dizzy
In such rarified Atmosphere.
As each year comes along,
I'm filled with pleasure —
Like finding Treasure!
 My day in January?
     Oh, I never tell.
It's on the same day of the week as Christmas
Exactly four weeks later,
Right in the middle of the January Thaw.
Which year?
     Ah, I never tell!
But I'm really very young —
It's only seventy years
Since I turned sixteen!
     There! Mother would be pleased.

                    Ronde Alexander

Resources

AARP.ORG/Bulletin

Agronin, Marc E. M.D. *How We Age: A Doctor's Journey into the Heart of Growing Old*. New York: Da Capo Press, 2011.

Agronin, Marc E. M.D. *The End of Old Age: Living a Longer, More Purposeful Life*. New York: Da Capo Press, 2018. Dr. Agronin presents a new paradigm for aging and sees it as a positive stage of development and one that should be embraced, not avoided.

AIM Insights. "Retirement Starts. Then What?" Toronto, Ontario: AIM Funds Management, Inc.

Bateson, Mary Catherine. *Composing a Further Life: The Age of Active Wisdom*. Vintage Publishing, 2011.

Booth, Frank, M.D. Et al. "Waging War on Modern Chronic Disease: Primary Prevention Through Exercise Biology," *Journal of Applied Physiology*, 88, 2000.

Booth, Frank, M.D. and Maun Chahravarthy, "Cost and Consequences of Sedentary Living: New Battleground For an Old Enemy," *President's Council on Physical Fitness and Sports, Research Digest*, series 3, no. 16, March, 2002.

Bottom Line Books. *Secrets to Healthy Aging*. Stamford, Ct: Bottom Line, Inc., 2016. Helpful ideas particularly on strengthening relationships in later life.

Bratter, Beatrice and Helen Dennis. *Project Renewment: The First Retirement Model for Career Women*. Scribner, 2013.

Brown, Stuart. *Play: How it Shapes the Brain, Opens the Imagination, and Invigorates the Soul*. NY, NY, Penguin, 2009.

Buettner, Dan. *The Blue Zones: Lessons for Living Longer from the People Who've Lived Longest*, Washington, DC, National Geographic, 2010.

Cameron, Julia. *It's Never too Late to Begin Again: Discovering Creativity and Meaning in Midlife and Beyond*. New York: Tarcherperigee, 2016. A workbook based on the author's 25 year old teaching tool "The Artist's Way" that inspires and recovers individual creativity. Many examples are given and it is clear that creativity and purpose are not dependent on wealth.

Corbin, Charles B., Ph.D., et al. *Concepts of Fitness and Wellness: A Comprehensive Lifestyle Approach*. McGraw Hill Education, 11th Ed., 2016.

Didion, Joan. *The Year of Magical Thinking*. Vintage Publishing, 2012.

Didion, Joan. *Blue Nights*, Vintage Publishing, 2012.

Editors of Bottom Line. *Say No to Nursing Homes: Your Ultimate Guide to Worry-Free Aging and Independent Living.* Stamford, CT.: Bottom Line, Inc., 2016. 513 pages of up to date advice for aging well.

Erikson, Erik et al, *Vital Involvement in Old Age*, NY, Norton, 1986.

Financialmentor.com/free-articles/retirement-planning/5-essential-pre-retirement-planning-questions. "How to Properly Prepare for Retirement: 5 must-ask questions!

Global Wellness, https://www.globalwellnessday.org/about/what-is-wellness/

Hettler, Bill, M.D., *National Wellness Institute*, https://nationalwellness.org/page/six-dimensions/

Hinden, Stan. *How to Retire Happy: The 12 Most Important Decisions You Must Make Before You Retire.* New York: McGraw Hill, Fourth Edition, 2013. Focuses on financial decisions and is especially helpful in discussing how to decide where to live and the impact of serious illness striking one of a couple.

Hoffman, Ellen. "Rewards of Dancing as You Age: Dancing Regularly Can Help Revitalize Your Mind and Your Body." https://www.nextavenue.org/rewards-of-dancing-as-you-age/.

Hurme, Sally Balch. *Get the Most Out of Retirement: Checklists for Happiness, Health, Purpose, and Financial Security.* Chicago: American Bar Association, 2016. An AARP book that covers every question of retirement planning. Helpful for readers who like checklists and workbooks.

Kondo, Marie. *The Life-Changing Magic of Tidying Up*, Ten Speed Press; 1st edition (October 14, 2014).

Lachman, Margie, Ph.D. "Aging Under Control?," *Psychological Science Agenda*, 19 (1), 2005.

Landry, Roger, M.D., *Live Long, Die Short*. Austin, Texas, Greenleaf Book Group Press, 2014.

Liptzin, Benjamin, M.D. "A True Golden Age: Dr. Liptzin Says Getting Older Doesn't Have to Mean Getting Old," *Healthcare News*. Internet Business Solutions, May 2004.

Lyubomirsky, Sonja. *The How of Happiness: A Scientific Approach to Getting the Life You Want*. New York: Penguin Books, 2007. A workbook to help you change your thinking and find joy. This book is often recommended by experts in behavioral health.

Manson, Jamie. "Biblical scholar Sister Sandra Schneiders celebrates four milestones,"*Globalsistersreport.org*, January 25, 2017.

Martin, Patricia Peters, Ph.D. and Helene De Montreux Houston, M.S., *The Other Couch: Discovering Women's Wisdom in Therapy*. IN: NorLightsPress, 2015.

Martin, Patricia Peters, Ph.D. and Renee Forte, *Liars, Cheats, and Creeps: Leaving the Sociopath Behind*. IN: NorLightsPress, 2016.

Maurer, Robert. *One Small Step Can Change Your Life: The Kaizen Way*. NY: Workman, 2004.

Ryff, Carol D. "Beyond Ponce de Leon and Life Satisfaction: New Directions in the Quest of Successful Ageing," *International Journal of Behavioral Development*, 12:35-58., 1989.

Schlossberg, Nancy K., Ed.D. *Revitalizing Retirement: Reshaping your Identity, Relationships and Purpose*. Washington, DC: American Psychological Association, 2010. Dr. Schlossberg is an expert in transitions and guides readers as they assess their lives and prepare for retirement (or not!). She identifies the various paths retirees take.

Schlossberg, Nancy K., Ed.D. *Too Young to be Old: Love, Learn, Work, and Play as You Age*. Washington, DC: American Psychological Association, 2017. Dr. Schlossberg's 10th book. She presents a plan to age happily.

Smith, Emily Esfahani. *The Power of Meaning: Crafting a Life that Matters*. New York: Crown Publisher, 2017. A beautifully written, research based book that explores meaning and purpose in our lives which brings true happiness.

Smith, Hyrum W. *Purposeful Retirement: How to Bring Happiness and Meaning to Your Retirement*. Coral Gables, FL: Mango Publishing Group, 2017. Advice from the "Father of Time Management" on approaching retirement years with positivity and zest.

The On Being Project, https://onbeing.org

UCDavis Wellness, https://shcs.ucdavis.edu/wellness/what-is-wellness/

Vaillant, George. *Triumphs of Experience: The Men of the Harvard Grant Study*. Cambridge, MA., Harvard University Press, 2012.

World Health Organization. https://who.int/about/mission/en/

Zelinski, Ernie J. *How to Retire Happy, Wild, and Free: Retirement Wisdom that You Won't Get From Your Financial Advisor*. England: Visions International Publishing, 2009. Retirement wisdom that covers all aspects of a happy life.

Book Club Discussion Questions

1. Have you thought about retirement? If so, what are your thoughts?

2. What "vital" wellness dimensions do you hope to incorporate into your retirement?

3. Using Schlossberg's types of retirees, do you see yourself as a Continuer, an Adventurer, an Easy Glider, an Involved Spectator, a Searcher, a Retreater, or a combination of types?

4. What things will you consider when selecting a retirement location?

5. Have you ever experienced "ageism"? If so, in what way?

6. Did any story in *Well-Come to Retirement: Thriving in Your Third Act* especially resonate with you?

7. What do you think will be your greatest joys in retirement?

8. What do you think will be your greatest struggles in retirement and aging?

Acknowledgements

Once again, we have had the privilege of publishing a book at NorLights Press. Thank you, Sammie and Dee Justesen, for your encouragement and enthusiasm. We are so fortunate to have found you.

We thank our husbands and family for their boundless love and understanding patience as we worked diligently to interview people, conduct literature reviews, and read every article we could get our hands on about retirement, aging, and wellness.

We wish to thank our friends who encouraged us to write this book and the gracious people who agreed to be interviewed. Stories and names are shared with their permission, or disguised to protect anonymity. It isn't easy to share personal information, but each of your stories is filled with wisdom and solutions to the many challenges of aging: regaining what has been lost, reinventing oneself, making difficult decisions, staying connected, staying healthy, finding purpose and meaning, dealing with change, and staying positive.

We wish to thank the many authors and researchers who spearheaded the concept of positive aging and share our viewpoint that getting older isn't the end but the beginning of a wise and new adventure.

We're thankful for finding each other and sharing our love of story and how the wisdom contained in stories educates and heals. We thank our many patients over the years who taught us about the wisdom of our elders. We embrace the advice of a sage elder in our first book, *The Other Couch: Discovering Women's Wisdom in Therapy*, who wisely states, "Expect change, accept change, adapt to change, and don't whine."

We hope the stories in this book will decrease the fear of aging and encourage you to examine your life and create a satisfying, joyous third act.

About The Authors

Patricia Peters Martin, M.S., Ph.D. is a Phi Beta Kappa graduate of Georgetown University and holds a doctorate in clinical psychology from Purdue University. Dr. Martin has done research work at National Institute of Mental Health studying bipolar disorder and at the National Institute of Child Health and Human Development studying the effects of early environment on child development. She has taught and supervised graduate and undergraduate psychology students at Purdue University, Springfield College, Bay Path University, American International College, and Westfield State University. Dr. Martin has counseled thousands of people in her 40 years of clinical practice in New England and the Midwest. Her patient population includes children and families, individual adults, teenagers and couples. Dr. Martin also leads group psychotherapy with women who have been or are in abusive relationships. Dr. Martin is a guest speaker throughout the United States presenting topics on mental health issues and relationship violence. She has made numerous appearances as a commentator on the local affiliate of public television and as a guest columnist for a large metropolitan daily newspaper and its online affiliate. She is the co-author with Helene De Montreux Houston of *The Other Couch: Discovering Women's Wisdom in Therapy* and the co-author with Renee Forte of *Liars, Cheats, and Creeps: Leaving the Sociopath Behind*. She has been married 39 years to her husband James, and is the mother of four children and grandmother of three. She lives in Western Massachusetts and New Hampshire.

Helene De Montreux Houston, M.S., APRN obtained degrees at Columbia and Boston Universities, and has practiced psychiatric nursing for almost 50 years in metropolitan Springfield, Massachusetts. While at Columbia University School of Nursing she was inducted into Sigma Theta Tau. She has provided counseling and medication management to thousands of people in a largely underserved population. She has spoken widely on the efficacy of psychotropic medication and been a guest commentator on the local public television affiliate. While at Baystate Medical Center, Helene taught medical students (Tufts University) and physician's assistant students (Springfield College) and participated in multiple continuing medical educational programs, seminars, and grand rounds. In addition to psychopharmacology, Mrs. Houston has specialized in trauma work, mood disorders, codependency, and women's health. Helene is co-author along with Patricia Martin of *The Other Couch: Discovering Women's Wisdom in Therapy*. She has been married for 50 years to Whiting and is the mother of two daughters and grandmother to one grandson. She lives in Western Massachusetts and New Jersey.

Patricia Peters Martin and Helene De Montreux Houston

CPSIA information can be obtained
at www.ICGtesting.com
Printed in the USA
FFHW011406041118
49003704-53258FF

9 780997 683486